# LEFT UNITY

## About Policy Network

Policy Network is an international thinktank and research institute. Its network spans national borders across Europe and the wider world with the aim of promoting the best progressive thinking on the major social and economic challenges of the 21st century.

Our work is driven by a network of politicians, policymakers, business leaders, public service professionals, and academic researchers who work on long-term issues relating to public policy, political economy, social attitudes, governance and international affairs. This is complemented by the expertise and research excellence of Policy Network's international team.

A platform for research and ideas

- Promoting expert ideas and political analysis on the key economic, social and political challenges of our age.
- Disseminating research excellence and relevant knowledge to a wider public audience through interactive policy networks, including interdisciplinary and scholarly collaboration.
- Engaging and informing the public debate about the future of European and global progressive politics.

A network of leaders, policymakers and thinkers

- Building international policy communities comprising individuals and affiliate institutions.
- Providing meeting platforms where the politically active, and potential leaders of the future, can engage with each other across national borders and with the best thinkers who are sympathetic to their broad aims.
- Engaging in external collaboration with partners including higher education institutions, the private sector, thinktanks, charities, community organisations, and trade unions.
- Delivering an innovative events programme combining in-house seminars with large-scale public conferences designed to influence and contribute to key public debates.

www.policy-network.net

# LEFT UNITY

## *Manifesto for a Progressive Alliance*

**Marius S. Ostrowski**

policy network

ROWMAN &
LITTLEFIELD
—————— INTERNATIONAL

London • New York

Published by Rowman & Littlefield International Ltd.
6 Tinworth Street, London, SE11 5AL
www.rowmaninternational.com

Rowman & Littlefield International Ltd. is an affiliate of Rowman & Littlefield
4501 Forbes Boulevard, Suite 200, Lanham, Maryland 20706, USA
With additional offices in Boulder, New York, Toronto (Canada), and Plymouth
(UK)
www.rowman.com

**British Library Cataloguing in Publication Data**
A catalogue record for this book is available from the British Library

ISBN: PB 978-1-78661-295-3

**Library of Congress Cataloging-in-Publication Data**

LCCN: 2019956021

*Drum links, zwei, drei!*
*Drum links, zwei, drei!*
*Wo dein Platz, Genosse, ist!*
*Reih' dich ein in die Arbeitereinheitsfront,*
*weil du auch ein Arbeiter bist.*

So left, two, three!
So left, two, three!
Comrade, here's the place for you!
Come join the workers' United Front,
for you are a worker too!

—Bertolt Brecht and Hanns Eisler,
*Einheitsfrontlied* (1937)

# CONTENTS

# INTRODUCTION

**B**efore a crisis can be fully overcome, it must first be completely understood. This seemingly simple rule is easy to grasp in principle, but much harder to stick to in practice. Whenever we face any problem, our instinct is to fall back on what is familiar, to retreat to the safety of accepted views and tried-and-tested approaches. But doing so harbours no guarantee of success. It can prevent us from noticing important facts about the case, from making the right connections between them, from detecting their vital causes. It can stop us from seeing the problem in a way that illuminates what it is really about, and points the way towards a lasting solution.

To understand and overcome a crisis requires us, first and foremost, to be honest with ourselves. As we confront it, we must always remain open to the possibility that we might need to revisit and revise our most fundamental views about the world. Only in that way do we stand a chance of correctly diagnosing the nature of the crisis, critically considering the existing proposals for how to address it, and formulating positive alternatives that improve on them. Diagnosis, critique, and a positive alternative: three elements that must work hand-in-hand to shape our response to every crisis. The deeper and more all-encompassing the crisis, the likelier it is that in this response, we will have to break out of our accustomed ways, detach ourselves from our old assumptions, and strike out in search of a new way forward.

Progressive politics is currently facing just such a crisis. It is a crisis that is several decades in the making, and is marked by several trends. First came the 'crisis of social democracy': the steady shrinking of social-democratic ambitions to resist the neoliberal revolution in conservative politics and the capitalist economy, mirrored in social-democratic parties' electoral decline from an average vote share of 35-40% in the 1950s-1960s to nearer 25% today.[1] This was followed by the demise of the 'end of history': the challenging of the apparent 1990s consensus around liberal democracy and free-market capitalism in the aftermath of the late-2000s financial crisis and the insurgent return of authoritarianism after long years of subterranean dormancy.[2]

Both trends have helped bring about a political situation generally described using the shorthand term 'polarisation'.[3] Yet this description is not entirely accurate. At a very simple level, we can see this by tracing the development of party vote shares in elections in the main democracies of the global North. In recent decades, vote shares for social-democratic and Christian-democratic/liberal-conservative parties have noticeably declined. At the same time, especially in the last 10 years, they have risen dramatically for national-conservative and neo-fascist parties, moderately for greens and liberals, and slightly for socialist and post-communist groupings.[4] Seen in purely left-right terms, this has led to an internal recomposition of the right towards more extreme positions, and a fragmentation of the left towards both the centre and the extremes.

But what looks on the surface like a hollowing-out of electoral support for the centre-left and centre-right disguises a much deeper realignment of ideological and party competition. At heart, this realignment can be traced back to deep changes in the basic structures of our societies themselves. Since the start of the 20th century, but especially in recent decades, societies have become much larger: populations have grown in size and are more densely concentrated. They have also become more complex: their populations are ever more specialised and differentiated, more intricately organised, and use increasingly sophisticated technologies. And societies have become more fluid: their populations are less locally rooted, and more outwardly and inwardly interconnected and mobile.[5]

These trends have disrupted and dislocated people from their old and established social ties, often (but not always) followed by forming and embedding them in new ones. And where social ties have led, social values have followed. As 'traditional' communities have been eroded, pressure to conform to their norms has weakened. In turn, those who resisted and rejected them have created new groups and moral codes that sit at odds with—even invert—what went before. Many people are caught in transition, bridging older and newer identities, semi-isolated atoms searching for the reassuring safety of a community to home and validate them. And these trends have been far from uniform within or across societies. Some parts— some geographical areas, some demographic groups—have pulled ahead, while others have stayed behind.

For left and right, this has meant that partisan disputes within society have become semi-detached from their old dimensions of struggle. Ideology is no longer simply about criticising versus defending the capitalist economic system (i.e., class politics) or nation-state institutions (i.e., nationality), although both elements still play an important role. Rather, it has broadened to include other identities alongside them. The dissolution of traditional views about sexual and family life has added ideological dimensions around sex, gender, and orientation. Migration flows after the decline of European colonialism have fostered new dimensions around race and ethnicity, and transformed the ideological role of religion. And changing understandings of people's mental and physical capabilities have added ideological focuses on education, age, health, and disability.

These newer dimensions are often grouped together with nationality into a single overall 'cultural' dimension, to contrast with the 'economic' dimension of class politics. Together, these make up the well-known 'political compass': a horizontal axis of economic interventionism versus *laissez-faire*, and a vertical axis of cultural authoritarianism (which is broadly associated with nationalism, collectivism, value-monism) versus libertarianism (typically linked to internationalism, individualism, value-pluralism). As political movements and parties have started to take positions on the newer dimensions, the centre of gravity of ideological competition is shifting away from economic and towards cultural concerns. The left-right spectrum has begun to rotate away from the priority of the horizontal towards the vertical polarity. And as the spectrum turns, the ideological positions of movements and parties become twisted and stretched by pressures to transform their electoral identities. Those that adapt survive; those that fail perish.

In transformative times such as this, the progressive left has a particular responsibility to be alert to the new and constantly shifting terms on which ideological struggles are fought. This responsibility goes to the very core of what progressivism means. Progressives do not just observe the deep changes that take place in societies, but lead the way in responding to them. The idea of progress rests on the assumption that any change can turn (or be turned) into an advance: an improvement that builds on what has come before, either through natural evolution or conscious action. Progressives' default position is to welcome social changes, foster them, search out their advantages, and defend them against their detractors.

Of course, this does not mean that every progressive gives every change in society their blanket endorsement. Not every transformation is automatically an improvement. Indeed, many are not limited to clear individual effects at all, but give rise to a chain of disparate, more-or-less unforeseeable knock-on consequences. It is the progressive left's task to impose on such changes a clear vision of society, to steer them towards being amenable (rather than inimical) to improving people's lives. In doing so, the left also needs to be clear about its own position in such transformations. It must remain conscious of how far they jeopardise its own established assumptions—the positions it defends, the values it believes in, the groups and interests it represents, and the bodies and institutions it comprises.

This is a daunting task, but in the current crisis it is also an urgent one. Yet the left does not have to take it on wholly unaided. Every moment of social change, however dramatic and ground-breaking, carries the echoes of precedent to some degree. Certainly, not every change takes the form of a crisis, and not every crisis leads to a revolutionary rupture. But the course of social development is marked by enough points of discontinuity—to put it in general terms—that we can trace the parallels between successive transformations. The left has a proud tradition of poring over the theory and strategy that went into signal moments of change—the revolutions of 1789, 1848-9, and 1916-23, to name only a few. What worked and what failed: both have lessons to offer the contemporary left.

Obviously, the left needs to tread carefully in its appeals to history. It must resist the inclination to look for timeless truths or easily transferable guidelines that tell us how (not) to act today. Context matters, and for every point of similarity between the present and the past, there are always differences that must also be taken into account. No two parts of society are quite the same. People and the social groups they belong to, the institutions that shape their lives, their ideas and motivations, their behaviour, differ over time and from place to place in ways that can be more or less subtle or extreme. It is possible, but by no means straightforward, to draw skilful analogies between them, and recycle their insights and experiences for our present needs. In this light, the left has to stay sensitive to how it can find the *right* moments and cases to compare with one another, and how far differences of time and space limit our ability to recapture the ideas of the past for our present purposes.

There are a few precepts that can help today's progressives learn from history. First and foremost, the left should avoid focusing only on top-level leaders and dramatic moments when it surveys the past. Rather, with the gaze of the social historian, it must look at how ordinary leftists coped with the prolonged, draining uncertainty that takes up most of the time during periods of transformation. Next, the left should not buy into received stories of inevitable success and failure. The aims and aspirations of its predecessors are no less valid for having been neglected or defeated, and projects of rediscovery are made all the more robust by choosing to learn from all aspects of their legacy. In the same vein, the left cannot treat the ideas and events of the past as limited only to their immediate contexts. Past progressives harboured hopes not just for their own times, but also for how they might influence the future, and by appropriating their work we are helping to realise their anticipated contribution.

The left must also not forget that, almost by definition, these same progressives were at least trying to be ahead of their times. Our rediscovery today should focus on leveraging their radical spirit, rather than getting lost in the (now quite possibly reactionary) details of what they thought and did. And finally, the left must remember that history always at least partly includes the more-or-less continuous evolution of meanings over time. It is thus called to reflect on which accumulations or breaks in meaning were 'good' or 'bad' from its contemporary vantage-point, and which should be kept, abandoned, or retrieved for its present purposes.

All in all, this goes to show that the left does not have to confront its present crisis blind. That is perhaps just as well, since the major precedent we have for what can happen in situations where the left is fragmented and the right has turned towards extremism forces us to return to one of the darkest periods in world history. The years between WW1 and WW2 were the first to see the rise of a new radical ideology on the right (fascism), the schism of a left damaged by acquiescence to conservatism into moderate and radical variants (social democracy and communism), and the nadir of a disoriented liberalism forced to revise its long-held assumptions. The eventual upshot was bloodshed and destruction on a systematic scale never seen before.

In light of this, it is fair to say that the left can do with every scrap of guidance it can get. For the left, the primary lesson from the interwar years is that of the sheer cost of disunity. Social democrats and communists spent the best part of two decades at each other's throats, the former decrying the despotic barbarism of 'Bolshevism', the latter dismissing the parliamentary road to socialism as 'social fascism'. By the time they switched to collaborating with each other and with liberals and centrists to avert the fascist threat, their divisions had become too acutely entrenched to prevent fascism's ascendancy. In amidst the carnage of war and genocide, the result was the near-total obliteration of an entire generation of left thinkers and activists—a loss from which the movement never truly recovered.

Yet throughout the interwar years, there was also no shortage of attempts to overcome these divisions and bring about left unity. From the first years after WW1, prominent voices across Europe preached and practised cooperation and compromise across the left's ideological divides. They urged parties to put aside differences on nationalism versus internationalism, rule by workers' councils versus parliamentary democracy, and welfare capitalism versus socialisation, in favour of working together to rebuild Europe after four years of war. Later, they pushed for progressive forces to ally under the banner of the 'united front' (across the working-class left) or 'popular front' (including the liberal centre) to fight against fascism taking hold.[6]

The left today must invoke the spirit of its last major struggle against the extreme right. It needs to recover the spirit that motivated the unifiers, not the dividers, of the past. The left must unite so that it is not exhausted by inward-facing competition before it even gets to the greater struggles with ideological entities beyond its borders. It cannot afford to waste activists and resources on litigating differences that are often of degree rather than kind, especially when viewed from the macroscopic perspective of the full range of the available spectrum. It must be able to offer a solid front to resist any attempts by the right to undo the progressive achievements of the past, and plunge society into reactionary decay.

So far diagnosis and critique—now what of the positive alternative? The left needs clear visions and proposals to overcome its fragmentation, and face the tasks ahead strong and united. What follows here are ten ways in which the left can confront its current division. They are inspired by the spirit of past efforts to achieve left unity, but they are motivated by the needs and possibilities of the crisis the

left faces today. It is for progressives of all colours to learn from
them what they can before it is too late.

## NOTES

1. Andrew Hindmoor, *What's Left Now?: The History and Future of
Social Democracy* (Oxford: Oxford University Press, 2018); Michael
Keating and David McCrone, *The Crisis of Social Democracy in Europe*
(Edinburgh: Edinburgh University Press, 2015).
2. Francis Fukuyama, *The End of History and the Last Man* (New York,
NY: Free Press, 1992); Robert Kagan, 'The end of the end of history', *The
New Republic* 238(7), 23 April 2008; Fareed Zakaria, 'The end of the end
of history', *Newsweek* 138(13), 24 September 2001, 70.
3. Alan I. Abramowitz and Kyle L. Saunders, 'Is polarization a myth?',
*Journal of Politics* 70(2) (2008), 542-55; Joseph Bafumi and Robert Y.
Shapiro, 'A new partisan voter', *Journal of Politics* 71(1) (2009), 1-24.
4. Christopher Green-Pedersen, *The Reshaping of West European Party
Politics: Agenda-Setting and Party Competition in Comparative Perspective* (Oxford: Oxford University Press, 2019); Swen Hutter and Hanspeter
Kriesi (eds.), *European Party Politics in Times of Crisis* (Cambridge: Cam-
bridge University Press, 2019); Cas Mudde, *On Extremism and Democracy
in Europe* (Abingdon: Routledge, 2016).
5. Zygmunt Bauman, *Liquid Modernity* (Cambridge: Polity, 2000);
Ulrich Beck, Anthony Giddens, and Scott Lash, *Reflexive Modernization:
Politics, Tradition and Aesthetics in the Modern Social Order* (Oxford:
Blackwell, 1994).
6. David Blaazer, *The Popular Front and the Progressive Tradition:
Socialists, Liberals, and the Quest for Unity, 1884-1939* (Cambridge: Cambridge University Press, 1992); Helen Graham and Paul Preston (eds.), *The
Popular Front in Europe* (Basingstoke: Palgrave Macmillan, 1987).

# I

# The left in modern society

# THE LEFT

What does it mean to be on the left? There is no single answer to this question, and left-wing ideas and policies come in a vast array of different forms. Socialists and liberals disagree on what kinds of things people should be allowed to own for their private use. Social democrats and communists differ on how social change should come about: gradual reforms or revolutionary overthrow. Anarchists suspect others of being too comfortable with the coercive power of the state. Greens worry that the others are willing to sacrifice the long-term health of the environment for economic development. And feminists, anti-racists, and activists for queer, disabled, and other civil rights insist that visions of a decent society are incomplete if they do not consider the importance of personal identity.

But at their core, despite their differences, all of these variants of the left often come back to a simple general rule: fight for 'those without', and fight against 'those with' who harm 'those without'. 'With' versus 'without', advantage versus disadvantage, privilege versus underprivilege—that, for the left, is the core way to understand society.

The left applies this general rule in several ways. At the heart of all left thinking lies a concern about *power*: the means and resources we have at our disposal, the options and opportunities we have relative to others, and the abilities, capacities, or status we are granted and how we use them. The left fights for *empowerment*, and against *oppression*. It wants to see a world where access to and control over resources is broadly evenly distributed among people, and where opportunities are allocated to them in a balanced way.

The left also has a closely-related focus on the *structure of society*: the kinds of groups we belong to, how these groups are combined or divided from one another, whether they are arranged into 'superiors' and 'inferiors', and whether we are in charge or have to obey, whether we lead or follow. The left fights for *parity*, and against *hierarchy*. It aims to dissolve divisions and stratifications between groups, and ensure that nobody in society is permanently 'in authority' and everyone is placed on a level playing-field.

Both of these feed into the left's distinctive social *attitude*: how we view other people, how we see ourselves fitting with them into society, how we react to novelty and change, and how single- or open-minded we are about the value of our own views. The left fights for *recognition*, and against *discrimination*. It acknowledges that diversity is an inevitable fact of life and part of what makes us human, and sees difference as something that should be tolerated, welcomed, or even better celebrated.

These come together in the left's view of social *behaviour*: how we engage with other people, whether we relate to them as friends to help or enemies to destroy, whether we treat society as a race to be won or a shared project in which everyone should flourish, and what goals we aim to achieve. The left fights for *cooperation*, and against *competition*. It wants to avoid a world of hostile rivalries where the only concern is individual gain, and establish a society built on mutual partnership where people try do things for the benefit of everyone.

Underpinning these concerns are a consistent set of concepts and values, which the left uses to frame and orient everything it fights for and against. Its central value is *equality*: bringing about situations where people are of the same or similar standing in certain important respects, or by certain criteria of measurement. This stands in close proximity to *justice*: ensuring that people are treated and provided for fairly, adequately, and correctly, according to their rightful due. And it is also closely connected to *solidarity*: recognising the reciprocal bonds and shared purposes that tie people together, and their duties to support each other in their mutual common interest. The left dismisses any suggestion that people might be valued asymmetrically, any attempt to deny or deprive them of what they are owed, or to divide and break them asunder.

At the same time, the left is concerned with a particular understanding of *freedom*: emancipating people from being held under forceful control, and giving them opportunities to exercise conscious choice over their lives without arbitrary constraints or coercion. It is also committed to *pluralism*: acknowledging that people are separate individuals who belong to various groups, of which there are a great number in complex society, and encouraging people to foster the many heterogeneous and incommensurable aspects of their identities. Finally, the left aims for *progress*: pursuing the continuous onward advance of society by developing ever new and better ways to bring about improvements in people's lives. The left rejects efforts to dominate or restrict people's lives, subject them to the intrusions of totalising moral codes, or disregard their needs in the name of preserving the *status quo*.

So far what the left stands for, and against. We can see all of these elements at work in everything the left fights for—from campaigning for universal suffrage to eliminating the gender pay gap, from fighting for free state education and healthcare to ensuring that everyone has the right to marry and start a family with whomever they love. But it does not defend its concerns and values in isolation. By definition, the left stands in contrast—or indeed, in opposition—to the centre and the right. What differentiates them from one another? It would be easy to say that the right is nothing but the diametric opposite of the left, that it rejects what the left believes and embraces what it stands against. Likewise, it would be convenient to see the centre as merely populated by those who try to negotiate a route between the 'extremes' of full left- and right-wing commitments.

Yet doing so underestimates the independence, integrity, and sophistication of both right-wing and centrist traditions. Certainly, the right embraces hierarchy and competition, in contrast to the left, and it tends to oppose equality and pluralism in the name of principles such as order, faith, and tradition. But it also endorses its own understanding of empowerment, and often relies on substitute versions of concepts such as freedom, justice, or solidarity. Similarly, the centre does aim for an even balance between opposing left-right commitments, such as parity and hierarchy, or stability and change. But in its quest for compromise and moderation, centrism veers towards aligning with the left on issues such as recognition and cooperation, couched in alternative interpretations of fairness, pluralism, and progress.

In other words, ideological contests are as much about defending opposing principles as they are turf wars about winning ownership of the same ones.[1] In this context, it becomes all the more important for the left to know where the dividing lines lie between left, centre, and right. By virtue of what they stand for and against, different people and social groups are located more or less firmly in each of these three camps. The left needs to know who it will clash with, and who it will overlap with, and over which concepts and issues. Some will be their inveterate enemies, impervious to a reconciliation of any kind. Others will be more malleable, laying the basis for collaboration beyond the left's boundaries.

What decides whether someone is 'on' or 'of' the left? This is also not just a straightforward matter. It is obviously not the case that all 'those without' side with the left, while all 'those with' side against it. It is not guaranteed that 'those without' will necessarily fight for anyone but themselves, or that they will not collude with 'those with' in harming others who are 'without'—by mimicking the behaviour of the more privileged, failing to stand up for others in their own position, or actively 'throwing them under the bus' for their own advancement. Similarly, not all of 'those with' are determined to hurt 'those without', but may instead be prepared to support them against the others 'with' who are, even at their own social cost—by taking part in outreach programmes, giving to philanthropic or charitable causes, or 'fighting their corner' in places from which the underprivileged are excluded. In other words, as the saying goes, 'where you are from' can have surprisingly little bearing on 'where you are at'.

Far more than who we are, it is what we do that makes us left-wing. Of course, many of those who are oppressed, subordinated within hierarchies, discriminated against, or casualties of competition fight for themselves and others like them energetically. They form the core of what the left as a movement has always been about. But there are also those who are already empowered, leaders within hierarchies, widely recognised, and winners from competition who can—and recognise that they should—use their advantage to combat their advantage. These are *allies*, and the left needs them as well. It relies on those who fight for themselves, and others who fight for them. It has had plenty of each in its history, from male advocates of women's suffrage to white civil rights campaigners. It needs to keep space for them both today.[2]

The left must also remember that there are many different dimensions of oppression, hierarchy, discrimination, and competition that can harm 'those without'. Class and nationality have been joined as socially significant identities by sex and gender, sexual orientation, race and ethnicity, religion, education, age, health, and disability. As society becomes more complex, it is likely that even more will emerge. The left must remain vigilant to society's deep changes, and the new and reemphasised dimensions and priorities they can foster. And it must think carefully about how these *dimensions of personal identity* are used to divide 'those with' from 'those without', and what fighting for 'those without' means in each case.

Of course, these dimensions are not independent of each other. People's identities intersect, subtly and often. They can cross-cut or align with each other, mitigating or exacerbating one another's effects, and fluctuating in relative importance. They also exist and develop semi-independently, and intersections between them do not stay fixed but are constantly fluid as well. This can blur the picture somewhat, as it means that few people in any society are wholly 'with' or 'without', fully privileged and advantaged or fully underprivileged and disadvantaged. Many instead fall into some middle category: part-'with' in some respects, part-'without' in others. Some examples are so classic as to have become tropes in modern society: gay men or men of colour, women who are white or wealthy, highly-educated children or foreign nationals. They benefit from their power, hierarchical position, recognition, or wins in some areas, but suffer from oppression, subordination, discrimination, or losses in others. For people in these categories, the concerns and values of the left are only partly relevant insofar as they address the 'without' aspects of their lived experience.

There are two ways of reading such 'intersectionality', as this phenomenon is known.[3] Pessimistically, it means that many people can at best partly relate to the message of the left. They may be caught in the contradictory ideological pulls of the centre and the right as well, as they choose to protect and favour the advantaging 'with' side of their lives over the disadvantaging 'without'. As a result, the left cannot reliably predict which way such people will lean merely from their personal situation. The left reluctantly realised a century ago that it was unlikely to capture the entirety of the industrial working class. Since then, it has rarely if ever captured the majority, let alone the entirety of any disadvantaged or underprivileged group. The most it ever manages regularly is significant pluralities—in recent decades, most often among minority ethnic groups or younger members of the population. Overall, the left cannot afford to 'essentialise'—i.e., one-dimensionally characterise—anyone in society. It cannot assume that someone who is partly 'without' will fight with the left *even if they are one of the people the left is fighting for.*

More optimistically, it also means that there are many people in society who can potentially relate to the left's message on some level. They may be no less amenable to the left's concerns and values merely because it is not their own personal situation that is constantly and immediately at stake. Or rather, the left should not assume that they will be automatically hostile towards it because its programme challenges their privileged 'with' aspects. It has always had to reach beyond its core vote to achieve electoral success, making inroads among socially-conscious members of the middle and upper classes, home nationals, men, white people, heterosexuals, etc. In the same way, it must not rule out electoral appeals to people in these middle categories, at least to present them with the option of leaning left. But it does have to be sensitive and careful in crafting its messaging to them, rooting its appeal in the most promising 'without' aspects of their lives.

Potentially, the left is to be found everywhere in society. Being 'on the left' works at any social scale, large or small, no matter the context. Every group, every body has members who care about who holds power within it, how it is structured, and the attitudes and behaviour its members display. Any of them may have significant differences between 'those with' and 'those without'. And each of them may well have members 'with' who worry how these differences affect 'those without' in it, and members 'without' who are determined to change their situation. This means that being progressive, even radically so, can come in many forms. However incremental or microscopic, all of these forms can be mobilised by the left.

Yet the reverse is also true. Every group has members who are comfortable with the existing relations between 'those with' and 'those without', and seek to entrench them further. Or, more depressingly, it may have quite a few who are disengaged from questions of privilege and advantage, and from the tensions between 'those with' versus 'those without' entirely. But the left cannot fall into the trap of presuming that any of these will remain irremediably fixed in their relative stances. It should not accept that any parts of society are irretrievably hostile to or uninterested in the cause of 'those without', and impervious to being won over. By the same token, it should also not expect that any parts will be consistently on its side, and immune from being lost to its opponents. Allyship is a role that white, wealthy, straight, cis, ablebodied, native-born men are entirely able to fulfil. Meanwhile, there is nothing about the disadvantaged that makes them automatically immune to tendencies of sexism, racism, class prejudice, homophobia, transphobia, ableism, or xenophobia.

The left must constantly find opportunities to champion the issue of transforming relations between 'those with' and 'those without' throughout society. To do this effectively, it must be aware of where things stand now—what the balance is between the relative presence of left, centre, and right in different *domains of activity* in society. What people do in their social lives can be categorised according to which domain their activities most closely belong to, contribute to, or engage with. When they produce, consume, and exchange or distribute goods and resources, they are participating in the *economy*. Where they interact with the administration, regulation, and coercion or repression of people and groups, they are involved in the domains of *politics* and the *law*. If they are engaged in 'ideating' (i.e., thinking up and reflecting on) and communicating meanings and messages, they are contributing to *culture*. When they study or instruct others, they engage with the domain of *education*. And when they foster intimacy and friendship, or engage with their own and others' nurture and healthcare, they are involved in *caregiving* (the archetypical 'social' domain). Although together they make up what we know as 'society', these domains vary in extent and significance, and they are all quasi-autonomous of one another.[4] Like personal identities, they can cross-cut or align, support or contradict one another, and shift in relative importance.

The left has successfully entered some of these domains, and established a presence that is hard to dislodge. The economic left typically takes the form of labour activism, cooperative and non-profit business models, or ecological and international-development entrepreneurship. Beyond party structures, the left in politics is hampered by formal 'neutrality' requirements in (e.g.) the civil service, police and security, or legal system, though some progressive areas do exist (e.g., welfare and pensions administration, and family or environmental litigation). Culturally, the left enjoys a weak presence in press and broadcast media, but a somewhat stronger one in newer online/digital outlets. In education, the left is most visibly advanced by student activism, as well as progressive themes in certain subjects (usually from the arts, humanities, or social sciences). But nowhere is it even close to being in complete control. There are isolated cases—e.g., particular companies, universities, or charities—where some kind of left-wing dominance has been reached. But there are far more where the left is in the minority, and must try much harder to make its presence felt. At the extremes, the latter cases stretch to large swathes of these domains and entire categories of their institutions, representing whole industries, partisan movements, religious denominations, scholarly disciplines, and so on.

The left needs to consider very carefully who it should be fighting for in each of these domains. Who counts as 'with' and 'without' varies depending on what forms power takes in each one, what kinds of structures it features, and what attitudes and types of behaviour people exhibit within it. Depending on the context, the left will find itself fighting for consumers and lower-grade workers, citizens and lower-rank officials, students and junior teachers, children and parents, the frail and sick, lower-level doctors, lawyers, carers, and so on. Who it is fighting against, meanwhile, is anyone ('with' or 'without') complicit in the worst treatment of 'those without' in each domain: exploitation, repression, tyranny, bullying, abuse, maltreatment, neglect, and the like.

Altogether, the left's social concerns, its values, its engagement with the various dimensions of people's identity, and its presence in different societal domains are its four key components as an ideology and as a movement. They are related to one another in complex ways. The left's first task is to establish a broad equivalence between all of its different fights. It needs to bridge people's shared and differing experiences of oppression, hierarchy, discrimination, and competition wherever they take place in society. Left-leaning members of many different groups have to engage with and learn from one another to develop and elaborate the foundational principles of left morality and strategy. Only in that way can they constitute the left as 'the left'—as a relatively cohesive movement, rather than merely a disparate collection of vaguely parallel tendencies.

To help give these efforts a degree of permanence, the left needs dedicated bodies that bring together 'those without' and their allies among 'those with' in every social institution—in each company, firm, office, department, centre, etc., across all societal domains. Within each of these institutions, leftists who share a particular personal identity should aim to find ways of giving themselves as a group a more permanent form. They need to constitute themselves as a single entity rather than a disparate set of individuals, perhaps through a defined membership, with a specific name or label, or meeting in a designated space on a regular schedule, with the primary task of placing the group's members in close and familiar relation to one another. These bodies should be arranged into a federal structure that creates scalable vertical and horizontal connections between these bodies in all the different institutions in a domain, all the way up to the highest possible level within each one. These connections should also be geographical, from the local or regional level all the way up to the national tier. The aim of these bodies is to ensure that the left can intervene at every scale in an ever more complex society—that it has both the micro-level penetration and the macro-level harmonisation it needs to be an effective force in society.

## NOTES

1. Michael Freeden, *Ideologies and Political Theory: A Conceptual Approach* (Oxford: Oxford University Press, 1998); W.B. Gallie, 'Essentially contested concepts', *Proceedings of the Aristotelian Society* 56 (1955), 167-98.

2. Sara DeTurk, 'Allies in Action: The Communicative Experiences of People Who Challenge Social Injustice on Behalf of Others', *Communication Quarterly* 59(5) (2011), 569-90; Keith E. Edwards, 'Aspiring social justice allies identify development: A conceptual model', *NASPA Journal* 43 (2006), 39-60. Diane J. Goodman, 'Motivating people from privileged groups to support social justice', *Teachers College Record* 102(6) (2000), 1061-85.

3. Patricia Hill Collins and Sirma Bilge, *Intersectionality* (Cambridge: Polity, 2016); Ange-Marie Hancock, *Intersectionality* (Oxford: Oxford University Press, 2016).

4. Niklas Luhmann, Stephen Holmes and Charles Larmore, *The Differentiation of Society* (New York, NY: Columbia University Press, 1982); Steffen Roth and Anton Schütz, 'Ten Systems: Toward a Canon of Function Systems', *Cybernetics and Human Knowing* 22(4) (2015), 11-31.

# LEFT AGENTS AND ORGANISATIONS

If being 'on the left' means fighting for 'those without', then who is doing that fighting? Certainly, the core of the left as a movement is 'those without', disadvantaged and underprivileged, who fight for themselves and others like them, along with a penumbra of others 'with' who fight alongside them. But members of the left vary in the intensity of support they offer its programme, and take part in its fights in several different ways. At base, they may help create a background climate of acceptance and agreement with the left's concerns and values. They can offer intermittent backing through voting and making donations, or mobilise more frequently by joining in protests or volunteering for campaigns. They can help formulate policy and spread propaganda, or run for prominent strategic and leadership positions. These are all forms of left activism, in which every member of the left can participate.

Yet no matter how broad-based it is as a movement of activists, the left relies on a variety of dedicated agents to take the lead in pursuing its goals. The more the left penetrates into the many different parts of society, the greater its ability to intervene directly and immediately when issues of left concern arise within them. But if this intervention is left only to whoever in that area happens to be a member of the left, this intervention is forced to rely on the spontaneous proactive energy of possibly disparate groups of activists—which can surge up impressively but also quickly dissipate. Part of establishing a permanent left presence across society is thus also creating and entrenching certain social roles that are uniquely specialised in embodying left principles and pursuing left goals within their part of society. These agents act as fulcrums around which left activism in that part of society turns, or nodes on which it is concentrated. They lead left mobilisation and coordinate left solidarity, raising the visibility and effectiveness of the left's activities.

In our ever larger, increasingly complex and fluid societies, being an agent of the left can mean a growing variety of different things. There are still—appallingly—many manifestations of, and justifications for classism, sexism, racism, homophobia, transphobia, ableism, and xenophobia in modern society. This means that there are many different ways in which left agents can—must—be at the forefront of the fight for 'those without'. Leading collective bargaining to secure fair improvements in pay, conditions, or rights; raising progressive causes as policy-changing agenda items in decisive meetings in businesses, ministries, faculties, hospitals, and so on; offering support to victims of oppression, discrimination, etc., through psychological counselling or legal advice; acting as trustees and systematic conduits for financial and human resources; all are crucial ways for left agents to assert the left's claims on behalf of all those disadvantaged by certain aspects of their personal identity or their particular societal roles. Yet the task of left activism, and of the agents who carry it out, is ultimately shared across its different forms: left agents are there to *represent* the assortment of people and groups that make up the left.

What are the requirements for being a representative agent of the left? In general, the left should avoid imposing too many formal conditions that a person or organisation has to meet to count as a left agent. The left needs to be open and flexible about who leads and coordinates its activities, as the constant flow of changes in society will always create room for new methods of fighting for its many disparate causes. Of course, a basic cut-off point is that the left's agents must themselves be 'on/of' the left. They must belong to either 'those without' or their allies among 'those with' who fight for 'those without' as a whole. It is not enough for them merely to understand or sympathise with the left's concerns and values, as some in the centre or on the right with left-leaning tendencies do. That is not left agency or activism: mere sympathisers are not people on whom the left movement can consistently and implicitly rely.

To be effective, agents must be capable of representing the groups on whose behalf they are acting. Representation can take different forms. Agents *speak for* their groups whenever these cannot speak for themselves. In doing so, they *portray* their group's situation to those outside it. And they *present* this *again and again* to assert their group's cause. As spokespeople, depicters, and advocates, agents must be able to champion their group's concerns and values in any context, even where they themselves have nothing personally at stake. Among other things, this needs them to have a capacity for self-abnegating empathy that allows them to relate to the negative experiences of classism, sexism, racism, etc., even if they have never experienced it (or anything like it) themselves. They need to be responsive to the needs of those they represent—whether they are bound to stick to strictly-delineated remits and instructions as *delegates*, or they have the latitude to exercise their own judgment and pursue their own self-defined purposes as *trustees*.[1]

Agents' representative responsibilities take different forms depending on the domain in which they carry them out. In the economy, left agents aim to improve the place of 'those without' as regards their income and penalties (if applicable), the distribution of credit and debt, hiring and firing, consumer rights, and promotion opportunities. In politics and law, they seek to protect them in the allocation of sanctions and rewards, the codes and guidelines regulating people's conduct, and how the boundaries of groups and their activities are demarcated and policed. In culture, left agents attempt to define and conceptualise ideas that foster the inclusion of 'those without' and their perspectives, and formulate, disseminate, and transmit social messages to ensure they reach the widest possible audiences. And in education and caregiving, they set out to prevent and redress imbalances in the growth and training of 'those without', ensuring that they benefit from the best available opportunities for learning and skills enhancement, a nurturing, safe family environment, as well as healthy engagement with their friends and contemporaries.

To ensure their reliability, agents need to be subject to clear accountability mechanisms that keep them answerable to their groups. It is not enough for a person or organisation to self-nominate or self-appoint as a group's agent. Such unilateral declarations are acceptable for generic members of a movement, or for its sympathisers. But they lack the formal guarantees needed to connect a specific group with these specific agents, which opens the door to the possible illegitimacy of certain agents and the failure to adequately represent certain groups. As a result, every group needs to carefully and transparently specify the processes by which it chooses and mandates its agents—through election, selection, or otherwise—so it is clear who is (and who is not) a designated agent, who does (and who does not) represent them.

For the left, it is vital that, in each case, agents specify concretely which particular part of the left they represent. What combination of 'those without' and 'those with' 'their' group comprises; what forms of oppression, hierarchy, discrimination, and competition they are concerned with; what understandings of equality, justice, solidarity, freedom, pluralism, and progress they hold; which dimensions of identity they focus on and which societal domains they operate in: all are key to defining 'their' left grouping. Left agents cannot just be abstract 'ambassadors-at-large' for the left movement as a whole. Who precisely they are speaking for, whose situation they are portraying and constantly re-presenting, and who gives them their mandate decides how widely their activities can be extrapolated to the left in general. The more specific the group, the more plausible and trustworthy their agents are *as* agents.

It is fairly rare for the left's agents to be entirely free-floating ideological entrepreneurs. Much more commonly, they are grouped into organisations that support and facilitate their activities on behalf of 'their' left groups. There are obviously many different categories of representative organisations of the left, some of which are extremely familiar to most people: political parties, trade unions, thinktanks, charities, pressure groups, non-governmental organisations, and so on. Their activities usually specialise within one societal domain, and many of them are associated with one specific aspect of personal identity—although some (e.g., parties, charities) bridge both identities and domains where these intersect or overlap. As a general rule, the more long-standing the left's preoccupation with a particular dimension of people's identity, and the more entrenched its presence within a societal domain, the more systematic and sophisticated the relevant form of left agency and activism becomes. The labour movement is a good example: in the 150-plus years since its first emergence, its activism has proliferated into a network of well-entrenched trade unions of different sizes, each specialised in a particular professional sector, along with a healthy contingent of labour/workers' parties. This stands in contrast to the smaller range of NGOs and charities that have emerged to cater to (e.g.) trans or disabled interests, and their near-nonexistent political equivalents. In other words, the 'centre of gravity' of left activism essentially tracks the recent history of society's evolution. Like all social movements—although perhaps to a lesser degree—the left slightly lags behind society's very latest developments.

These organisations, on aggregate, are the most immediately visible manifestations of the left as a movement. They frame its members' voting and donation options, steer its protests and campaigns, shape its policies and messaging, and provide its strategic leadership. Of course, the left as a whole is far larger and more diverse. But its social presence is heavily dominated by these representative organisations in a way that paints a somewhat asymmetric picture of the concerns and values of the left taken together. The danger is that these more established organisations crowd out newer and less formalised sites of activism. So if the left is serious about treating dimensions and domains as being of equivalent importance, it needs to prioritise developing the quantity and quality of its activism in more marginalised, insurgent areas.

No single representative agent or organisation has a monopoly on the 'left' label. For that matter, no agent or organisation has a necessary or automatic claim to be 'left' at all. Activism on any personal dimension or in any societal domain can come from the centre and right as well as the left. It is not any more authentically left just because it focuses primarily on (e.g.) gender, ethnicity, or class, or is active mostly within politics, the economy, or education, and so on. Of course, the left includes agents and organisations that fight for the poor/deprived, which are feminist/gendered, anti-racist/decolonial, LGBTQ*-oriented, environmentalist, republican/democratic, etc. But what makes them representative of the left (as opposed to the centre or the right) is an explicit and sustained mandate from left groups—from specific people 'without' and their allies—and an ongoing commitment to left concerns and values.

Further, the left should not assume that any of these agents or organisations are necessarily the sole representatives for 'their' left groups. First, the left's representatives do not control the left as a movement: that assumption reverses the direction of accountability between the left and its agents. Agents derive their roles from the needs of specific groups within the movement: they do not decide, but merely reflect, these groups' concerns and values. As such, neither these groups nor the movement owe their agents anything in return beyond what they need to carry out their roles. Second, given the growing size and complexity of society, no single agent or organisation can fully speak for, portray, or present every aspect of 'their' group's situation in every context this requires. Representation relies ever more on specialisation, and the further society develops in this direction, the more closely-delimited left activism will become.

This does not just mean that there are many different organisations working to achieve the same left goals in different parts of society—although that is certainly the case. Beyond that, it means that because people have multiple dimensions to their identity, and because they are active in several domains at the same time, they will be represented several times over by organisations that reflect different aspects of who they are and what they do. For instance, a lesbian university student of colour from a Muslim background, who works a part-time retail job to pay her rent, and has to help care for her elderly relatives at home, would be 'claimed' as an example of someone 'without' who needs fighting for by left organisations in several societal domains, and ones focused on several different personal identities. Members of the left typically belong to more than one of the many overlapping groups within the movement, and they may be conscious of different aspects of their 'leftness' to varying degrees at different times. Not all left agents and organisations will be relevant to them. Some will only be significant to them at very specific points in their lives—e.g., when they vote in elections, donate to a charity, or go on strike with others in their company. Altogether, the relationship of the left movement to its agents is best viewed as a complex network of overlapping chains of accountability.

As a movement, the left plays a transformative role within society. From its agents' perspectives, this is not just a matter of achieving certain transformative priorities—alleviating certain concerns or realising certain values. What is also important is the way in which left activism carries out its task of transformation. Left agents face the choice between operating within society as it is, and prefiguring society as the left wants it to be (and everything in between).[2] This choice relates to the relationship between approaches and goals, means and ends: whether the former are merely the way to bring about the latter, or whether they need to reflect them as well. It is impossible for any single agent or organisation to bridge the full range of options implied by this choice. Each left group needs several parallel organisations to take up different 'positions' along the spectrum of possible approaches—even if, ultimately, they are all aiming for the same end goal.

The left needs some way to hold together the potentially very disparate approaches of its agents and organisations. What should unite them is that the left's 'versions' of how it represents the disadvantaged and underprivileged in the economy, politics, law, culture, etc., must in themselves reflect left concerns and values. The means the left uses to achieve its ends must themselves also empower people, ensure parity between them, and bring about their mutual recognition and cooperation. They must treat people equally and justly, bolster their solidarity, emancipate them, foster their plurality, and constantly aim for progress. Evidently, even within the parameters of left ideology, both these concerns and values are open to a range of interpretations. Part of the mandating and accountability processes for left agents must therefore be clear stipulations about how the left groups they represent expect their activities to reflect these concerns and values in practice.

This underlying consistency in concerns and values creates a sort of correspondence between otherwise separate agents and organisations in their activism on left groups' behalf. From this emerges the overarching characteristic of 'left-ness' for the movement as a whole. The more mutually complementary the activism of these agents and organisations, the more 'the left' is realised as an organic movement. In the absence of such correspondence and consistency, the left runs the risk of fragmentation. 'Those without' and 'those with' who stand alongside them become forced to choose between different parts of their personal identities or social engagements. They are forced to mandate representatives who bear little relation to one another, but who still lay claim to their support. Where such lax disconnection sets in, different strands of left activism become mutually exclusive, even contradictory, as agents and organisations no longer help each other's efforts but start to undermine them instead.

Together, whether harmoniously or dissonantly, all the agents and organisations that represent the left play a defining role in giving it its immediately discernible character as a movement. In view of this, the left needs to make the connections between them more inclusive and systematic. To streamline their activism on behalf of 'those without', it must develop mechanisms to coordinate their representative activities across the different dimensions of identity they focus on and the domains in which they operate. In doing so, it has to balance two aims. Its agents have to be able to pursue independently the tasks 'their' left groups have mandated them to perform. And, at the same time, they need to be kept acutely attuned both to other agents' activities, and to the development of the left movement as a whole.

At the moment, the relationship between the left's organisations is highly asymmetric. Parties and unions currently largely dominate the other organisations, with (especially) thinktanks and pressure groups essentially subordinated to them as affiliates or satellites—e.g., as with the culture of fringe events at party conferences. This is a poor reflection of the diversity of agency within the left movement. The left needs an overarching body that can reflect and represent it as a movement as a whole: a forum that can bridge the specialised divides between its different representative agents and organisations. Such a body would act as a second tier of mandating and accountability, with delegates to it chosen by, and from among, the agents in each representative organisation. This body would thereby be indirectly accountable to the left's various constituent groups. It would thus be deliberately and consciously designed so that left agents can speak for, portray, and re-present 'their' group's situations and priorities before an audience representing the left movement as a whole.

## NOTES

1. Anthony Harold Birch, *Representation* (London: Macmillan, 1972); Hannah F. Pitkin, *The Concept of Representation* (Berkeley, CA: University of California Press, 1967).
2. Carl Boggs, 'Revolutionary process, political strategy, and the dilemma of power', *Theory and Society* 4(3) (1977), 359-93; Uri Gordon, 'Prefigurative Politics between Ethical Practice and Absent Promise', *Political Studies* 66(2) (2017), 521-37.

# PARTIES AND PARTISANSHIP

**A**lthough its activism touches many areas of social life, the left is associated especially strongly with politics—specifically, electoral campaigning and mobilisation, and wielding the machinery of governance. Parties are the dominant left organisations that represent 'those without' and their allies in the political domain—and partisanship is the main mode in which the political left engages its rivals in the centre and on the right. In general terms, parties join together several types of political agents who share the same focuses on social concerns, and the same understanding of social values, ranging from rank-and-file party members and campaigners to election candidates and party officials. What distinguishes such 'partisans' as specifically *political* is that they operate mainly within institutions and processes of social administration and coercion. Their mandated task is to fight for 'those without' at the level of public policy, through legislation, executive authority, bureaucratic implementation, and police/military enforcement.

Political parties and their agents have a number of different purposes. They regulate and clarify the ideological distinctions between different groups across the left-right spectrum, institutionalising pluralism in the form of *factionalism*. Parties are among the primary exponents of specific political ideologies: liberal parties typically champion liberalism, occasionally with a side of social democracy; social-democratic parties embody social democracy, with 'wings' of liberalism and socialism; green parties advance green ideology, usually with social-democratic and liberal undercurrents, and so on. They provide frameworks to corral, channel, and systematise political agents' energies and activities, and to recruit and engage members of the population. Parties issue programmes and manifestos that summarise the shared outlook of the agents they join together in a defined geographical area and at a certain point in time. And they coordinate propaganda efforts to spread the particular way they focus on social concerns and interpret social values, often distilled into shorthand symbols for easy recognition and consumption (e.g., through rosettes, logos, and flags).[1]

While these purposes have remained largely consistent, political parties are undergoing some major changes in their structure and role. The most marked change has been the decline of a holistic 'catch-all' logic in their appeal.[2] Since the electoral franchise began to be extended to the entire adult population in countries across the world in the late 19th and early 20th centuries, many parties of left, centre, and right adopted 'big tent' approaches to capturing the concerns and values of broad swathes of their electorates. As society has become more complex, ideological diversity has vastly increased due to the rising significance of new dimensions of identity. These dimensions have jostled for political empowerment and recognition, and catch-all parties were faced with a growing need to accommodate them to keep securing winning voter coalitions. But the sheer speed and extremity with which these cross-cutting identities proliferated into sectional interest-advocacy groups, often accompanied by new and complex factional rivalries, outstripped catch-all parties' capacity to adapt and respond in a way that kept 'their' voters adequately unified.

Instead, there has been an increasing emergence of parties with the specific rationale of representing particular interests and identities. Essentially, these mirror the growing number of salient ways in which the *status quo* can be read and understood, even from within the same broad ideological perspective, and the fragmentation of both consensus with it and dissensus from it. In place of a holistic 'catch-all' logic, parties' appeal increasingly derives from a partial logic of 'preference-satisfaction'.[3] Rather than claiming to reflect the population as a whole, parties reflect the different ways in which it can be divided based on various demographic criteria. As personal identity becomes ever more politicised, the line between identity and cause, or interest, is being blurred. Partisanship is moving towards the assumption that 'demographics is destiny'—that people ('with' or 'without') fight above all for themselves, to maintain or improve the social situation they are in based on who or what they are.

As a result, the parties that exist already have gradually retreated in their representative ambitions as their electoral success has faltered. Meanwhile, new 'single-issue' parties have emerged that blur the line between parties *per se* and related organisational types, such as lobbying or special-interest groups. Green parties are the obvious example, with a primary focus on environmental policies. Others have emerged as well, including regional-nationalist and ethnic minority parties, 'grey' parties representing pensioners and the aged, 'women's equality' and other feminist parties, and 'pirate' and other anti-corruption parties who defend civil liberties. These parties have been more or less successful at establishing themselves, depending on the rules of each country's electoral system. But in general, people across the left-right spectrum have developed more and more options for where they can turn to express their ideological commitments—as voters, members, campaigners, and so on.

The effect has been the emergence of a kind of division of labour between parties clustered at various points on the ideological spectrum. Parties increasingly place their own emphases on different aspects of an (often implicitly) shared programme. As a result, they become even more specialised. As representative organisations, they are already predominantly active within the political domain. Now, they steadily shift from trying to institutionally align their approaches to people's various identities towards instead dividing along the fault-lines between them as these identities cross-cut.

Where formerly liberal or social-democratic parties would have sought to 'bridge' all the claims of different classes, regions, ethnic groups, age groups, and so on, they increasingly 'pick their battles' when vying for support among the electorate, ceding whole constituencies to (e.g.) greens or regional nationalists. Certainly, political parties generally still try to have *some* position on every identity-related social issue, but these are increasingly peripheral formalities around ever-more particularised cores. In other words, the intersections of identity are gradually being entrenched as a source of political division, rather than a gateway to political cooperation. Yet the majoritarian logic of electoral politics has not changed. Minority governments lack legitimacy and stability in democratic systems: they have difficulty passing legislation, and their authority, implementation, and enforcement measures are liable to subversion and resistance. As a result, the rise in party fragmentation and proliferation merely raises the likelihood of (and need for) cross-party alliances. This, at the political level, is one of the core bases of the need for left unity.

Moving beyond parties and partisans, the changing character of parties has moved in parallel with changes in how people support them. This is especially obvious in the case of voters. There has been a gradual decline in party loyalty and tribalism, and an increase in 'swing voting' and claims of 'independent' status. Voting is becoming less an expression of a deep and consistent social identity, and more a 'pick and mix' approach to policy preferences and preoccupations at a particular point in time. This should not be seen as evidence that voters are becoming any less committed to their concerns or values. Rather, they are becoming more aware of the complexity of own personal identities, and are choosing to shift emphases between different parts of them, from one dimension to another.

Similar changes are also increasingly at work in how people treat party membership. If voting is about a one-off choice of candidates in an election, membership is about signalling a more sustained commitment to the particular constellation of political concerns and values a party stands for. With only rare exceptions, there has been a long-term decline in the percentage of the population who are members of political parties.[4] Parties' response to this decline has been to reduce or discount membership dues, introduce tiered membership types (affiliation, 'registered supporters', mailing lists, etc.) with differential rights and obligations, and integrate digital and online technologies to boost partisan 'sign-up'. In parallel, parties have shifted to rely on other sources of income (e.g., donations, fundraising, state funding), and radically transformed their campaigning methods to make them less labour-intensive (e.g., by subcontracting out the creation of party materials, relying on a mobile targeted core of professional partisans). All such moves are designed to lower the entry costs and barriers to this comparatively low-intensity form of partisan agency.

As a result, both voting and party membership are losing their stringency as forms of ideological commitment. Both have become increasingly decoupled from more intense types of electoral activism (e.g., campaigning, fundraising), and are turning more into 'passive' signals of principled commitments. This changes the stakes for the relationship between people and parties as representative organisations, especially regarding agreement or disagreement over the concerns and values expressed in party policy and strategy. Joining and leaving parties is no longer as costly or as stigmatised, since the proliferation of nearby alternatives gives highly-politicised people a greater choice of plausible venues for their activism. In many European systems, the left of the party system has at least three or four out of left-liberal, social-democratic, left-regional-nationalist, green, and post-communist parties available for left activists and voters to oscillate between. Alternatively, in plenty of cases, dissenting party members do not leave but quietly cast their vote elsewhere to send a signal to their own party that ideological change is needed. In short, switching away from a party is no longer tantamount to abandoning an entire wing of the ideological spectrum.

Left parties need to adapt to these new political logics. At the moment, many left parties are torn between operating a near-totally exclusive membership policy, whereby someone can only be a member of a single party at any time—except in a few select cases, such as the Cooperative Party or the Women's Equality Party in the UK—and the need to amass material and manpower resources that they can deploy for effective large-scale campaigning. These parties are also torn between a fetishistic preference for 'lifelong' consistent voters and a correlative tendency to see 'vote switching' as a sign of treachery or unreliability, and the electoral need to appeal to 'swing voters' to bolster their baseline or core support, and achieve electoral pluralities and majorities. Both of these tensions punish people who are clearly 'on' or 'of' the left, but whose concerns and values do not easily align with those of any single party—or bridge those of several parties—forcing them to choose between parties that they could otherwise simultaneously support.

Left parties also have an unjustified preference for long-time members, on the principle that loyally belonging to a party is a sign of not only organisational but also ideological diehard commitment, and thus to be rewarded. They also have a correlative tendency to condemn new members in terms of 'entryism'—an underhand attempt to 'infiltrate' the party organisation in order to manipulate and undermine the party's ideological direction. Given the sheer proliferation of left parties that people can potentially join, it is not clear that the duration of their membership of one left party is a relevant indicator of their broader left conviction. 'Keeping the faith' and the 'zeal of the convert' are both useful and necessary aspects of any party's membership. Decoupling the necessary link between left party membership and 'left-ness' also cuts the other way. Like any organisation, once a party organisation has been set up, its social concerns and values can 'drift' significantly from where it started out. It is only the choices of people on the left to lend or withhold their support from it that can ensure that a nominally left party and its members continue to formally and explicitly seek their legitimacy from the left in society.

Within the wider ecosystem of the left's representative agents and organisations, parties are actually quite unusual in their approach, especially in their exclusivism about membership. Beyond the political domain, other left organisations (unions, thinktanks, media outlets, etc.) are not as restrictive about who can be a subscription member—i.e., who can participate in 'their' organised activism on behalf of left concerns and values. From this perspective, party factionalism actually stands in the way of maximising parties' activist capacity. It limits the transfer of material and manpower resources between different parts of the left (e.g., between workers', green, or regional-nationalist parties). Worse, such factionalism leads to ineffectual and wasteful deployment and mobilisation of activists and resources. This is especially the case where internecine left party-on-party contests in electoral campaigns 'crowd out' the left's focusing on the 'real enemy' in the centre or on the right.

This is greatly damaging to the left as a cohesive movement. It forces left agents to prioritise their organisational membership over their belonging to the left, and often to choose between different salient aspects of their own personal identity—class versus gender versus ethnicity, etc. It is also fundamentally an 'un-left' approach. It goes against the left's foundational preference for cooperation over competition, as well as the left's embrace of tolerant ideological pluralism and rejection of totalising monism. Ultimately, it may—and historically, often has—cost the left not only votes but also seats, especially in countries with electoral systems that rely heavily on geographical constituencies. If left votes are factionally divided between several parties while the centre and right are more united, this can deprive the left of electoral victories even where it is in the majority among the relevant electorate.

This also means that the left cannot lose sight of what electoral system it is operating in. In many electoral contexts, voters only have one vote to cast; in a few, they have two or more (e.g., constituency plus regional/national list, or 'split ticket' voting). This usually forces left voters who are not neatly partisan to 'pick a side' and prioritise some of their own concerns and values over others. Of course, the left should push for innovative electoral amendments that allow voters to spread their preferences in a way that more accurately reflects their own ideological positions (e.g., multiple votes per voter, fractional votes). But failing these, the left as a whole urgently needs to avoid destructive electoral competition between left parties as far as possible.

Another part of this, continuing on from the need to end the domination of left parties over other left organisations, is for the left to recognise the autonomy these organisations have over their choice of political affiliation. The left needs to break the automatic affiliation link between select left parties (usually social-democratic workers' or labour parties) and other left organisations—especially trade unions and thinktanks, though the latter are often fairly adept at cross-party collaborations and crossovers. Like parties, these other representative organisations can also 'drift' in their constellation of social concerns and values after they are set up. Insofar as they still carry the mandate of 'their' group within the population, they need to be free to reaffiliate to other parties. Ideally their new parties will be on the left if they are still themselves representative of left groups—but the left also needs to accept that these other organisations are as likely to 'drift' towards the centre and right as parties themselves are.

In a similar vein, the left must recall that representative agents and organisations do not control the left groups whom they represent. There is no obligation as such for left-leaning people to support any given left party as voters, or join it as members or other partisans. With the new proliferation of available parties, they can afford to be more selective, and choose the party that best reflects their concerns and values, given their personal identity and societal engagements. In other words, by implication, no left party has an automatic right to keep existing. For instance, just because for over 100 years it has traditionally been workers' or labour parties who 'led' the left side of the party spectrum does not mean that their position of primacy could (or should) not be 'usurped' by liberal, green, or regional-nationalist parties. In order to confirm their legitimacy as still the best political representatives of 'their' part of the left movement, parties have a responsibility to constantly reprove their representative capacity and accountability. They need to demonstrate that they are still able—ideally, the most able—to speak for, portray, and re-present the political concerns and values of 'their' left groups. And they have to show that they are still bound by a clear and effective accountability link to 'their' left groups. They need to be able to demonstrate that their political agency is still dependent on the people they are fighting for, and not independent of their needs and interests.

Ultimately, the danger of party factionalism is that it stands in the way of left ideological evolution and innovation. Given the changing character of partisanship, there is no guarantee that any single party can reliably and consistently take the lead in advancing the left's political representation as a whole. The left must remain open to the idea that the next 'best' left response to deep social changes can come from anywhere in the movement. As a result, the left needs to open up the flow of debate, mutual influencing, and engagement between parties on questions of policy and strategy, not encourage entrenchment into partisan side-taking for its own sake. It must not misconstrue the level at which defence or ownership conflicts over left principles should be taking place. It does not get the left anywhere if these conflicts are internal—rather, it must remember that its greatest clashes, and the most determined challenges to its social concerns and values, lie to the right (and centre).

Given how central political activism is to the left as a movement, it is especially important for it to find a way to minimise electoral attrition between its various political parties. The left needs to accept that, in contemporary, highly-complex society, there are now multiple parties that can legitimately represent the left as political organisations. Consequently, the left needs to change party rules to allow left supporters among the wider population and their partisan agents to join more than one party as members. If a leftist voter or activist feels equally drawn to (e.g.) a liberal, workers', and green party, they should be able to join all three without fear of rejection or expulsion. This would be a fairly straightforward way of overcoming the divides that complex societal specialisation has brought about, and creating bridging opportunities that can help maintain at least a loosely cohesive political left presence. It would be an effective institutional way of ensuring that the constituent groups that make up the left movement have their concerns and values reflected as effectively and completely as the movement's political presence allows.

The greatest benefit of such a change for left parties would come from the pooling of otherwise rivalrous resources: finances from dues payments, activist manpower, proprietary ideas, and the like. It is a micro-level change that would have major ramifications for reducing left-on-left political competition and correlatively fostering cooperation—e.g., through 'joint-ticket' parliamentarians and other elected officials strengthening the left's position versus the centre and right in local and constituency contests. It would by no means eradicate differences between parties, in the sense that each of them would still be able to advocate for their own unique ideological focus on social concerns and the interpretation of values. But it would prevent social complexity from turning into political 'siloisation' or 'Balkanisation' for the left as a whole.

## NOTES

1. Nancy L. Rosenblum, *On the Side of the Angels: An Appreciation of Parties and Partisanship* (Princeton, NJ: Princeton University Press, 2010); Jonathan White and Lea Ypi, *The meaning of partisanship* (Oxford: Oxford University Press, 2016).

2. André Krouwel, 'Otto Kirchheimer and the Catch-All Party', *West European Politics* 26(2) (2003), 23-40.

3. Cees van der Eijk *et al.*, 'Cleavages, Conflict Resolution and Democracy', in Mark Franklin *et al.* (eds.), *Electoral Change: Responses to Evolving Social and Attitudinal Structures in Western Countries* (Cambridge: Cambridge University Press, 1992), 406-31.

4. Ingrid van Biezen and Thomas Poguntke, 'The decline of membership-based politics', *Party Politics* 20(2) (2014), 205-16; Peter Mair and Ingrid van Biezen, 'Party Membership in Twenty European Democracies, 1980-2000', *Party Politics* 7(1) (2001), 5-21.

# II

# Left cooperation

# THE POSSIBILITY AND NECESSITY OF COOPERATION

In the current context of societal fragmentation and polarisation, an ever more central concern for the left is the tension between cooperation and competition in social behaviour. Specifically, when and where in society is cooperation possible, and necessary? Certainly, we can think of historical moments and situations of greater ideological consensus, not just on the left, but also with the centre and right: the rise of the welfare state as a point of common ground between socialism, liberalism, and Christian democracy; the 'post-war consensus', which held together ideologies as far apart as conservatism and social democracy; or the 'neoliberal consensus', which spilled over from conservatism and libertarianism to shape and coopt liberalism and social democracy. But these have not always been the case. The rising existential threat of the far right, and the growing presence of racist, sexist, homophobic, and other similar social forces determined to destroy the left as movement and frustrate its goals, makes it all the more important to consider how and where the left can find partners for mutual support and society's benefit.

The centrality of the left's fight for cooperation and against competition does not necessarily entail downplaying or excluding its other social concerns. Rather, they are all closely interrelated. Forming close partnerships for common purposes and taking one another's side as friends (even if only on specific issues) collectively empowers people, not least by pooling their resources and enhancing their social presence. Mutuality between cooperation partners breaks down asymmetries between them, and shares authority out among them more evenly on the basis of parity. And cooperation for joint benefit is premised on taking into consideration all sides' different needs and interests, which guarantees them at least a defined context in which they are fully recognised. In other words, by pursuing cooperation, the left is not detracting from, but rather also fostering its other concerns.

What does cooperation mean in practice? Fundamentally, it rests on the pursuit of joint projects undertaken on a collective basis to achieve shared aims. Within this, cooperation can mean sharing control and leadership, via joint executive committees or boards, co-chairs with agreed sharing of responsibilities, or mutual veto arrangements. It can involve pooling material and manpower resources, such as exchanging canvassing data, sharing activists for campaign mobilisation, or mutual financial support. It may rely on people exchanging and communally deliberating on ideas, in more-or-less formal conferences and forums, cross-party bill drafting, or collaborative policy proposals. Cooperation may also require people to abide by common rule-frameworks, such as explicit statements of principle, practical guidelines, or deferring to mutually-agreed disciplinary, monitory, or arbitration bodies. It may have people mutually supporting each other in skills and strategic training, from protest and bargaining tactics to rhetorical eloquence. Overall, cooperation entails a deep and continuous reciprocal involvement by several (groups of) people in the activities they engage in.

What cooperation means in any given situation depends on its context: different situations can require very different cooperative approaches. Cooperation can be highly specific and delimited to particular social concerns, values, dimensions of identity, or societal domains, depending on the precise remit of the situation the left confronts in each case. It can take the form of a cross-party commitment to end discrimination and bigotry against LGBTQ* people. It can come in the guise of trade unions agreeing a common policy for advancing fair treatment of workers in wage negotiations or employment tribunals. Cooperation can include rival civil rights and racial empowerment groups suspending mutual criticism in favour of working together towards achieving legislative reforms. Or it can involve teachers and academics from different disciplines exchanging suggestions for how to diversify the contents of their curriculums.

The decision over whether or not to cooperate chiefly depends on what is at stake in each situation. Some may require a heroic last stand against implacable foes; others patient consensus-building among open minds. The key constraint, however, is that left cooperation cannot be self-defeating. Any instance of cooperation can only take place in the interests of prefiguring and increasing cooperation in society at large. It also cannot come at the cost of other core left commitments, whether concerns or values—which means that, insofar as there is an essential disagreement about concerns and values at stake, cooperation cannot successfully take place. In other words, left cooperation requires a shared basis in at least broad-brush agreement on concerns and values; though some leeway must be left for differences between the cooperating elements, these need to be of degree, rather than of kind.

A vital part of any such decision is also an accurate and candid assessment of the balance of forces within the general population. Fundamentally, cooperation is premised on the assumption that unilateral or fully independent action is impossible or undesirable. If parties insist on LGBTQ* emancipation on their own terms exclusively, unions pursue conflicting tactics for supporting workers, civil rights groups make contradictory legislative demands, or teachers put forward wildly different proposals, they may not achieve their aims at all, but rather merely sow inconsistency and confusion with piecemeal half-measures. It could be a decision born out of necessity, due to the lack of majority support among the population, or the likelihood of majority resistance; or due to insufficient capacity, and a relative position of weakness. Or instead, cooperation could also be a decision resulting from strategic choice, a gesture of inclusive magnanimity despite majority support, barely-existent resistance, adequate capacity, or from a position of strength.

To make and justify its decision, the left needs to know where it lies relative to the centre and the right in and across all dimensions of identity and societal domains. At the moment, it clearly has a better idea of this on some fronts than others. For instance, though 'leftness' is roughly equal across men and women, the internal composition of left support is subtly gendered, with men more likely to lean liberal or left-radical, and women more likely to lean social-democratic or green.[1] Something similar happens with 'social grade' (a measure of class), where social-democratic left support typically captures a plurality or majority of lower grades, while liberal-dominated left support takes a relatively smaller share of higher grades.[2] Age tends to conform to the linear stereotype of people becoming more right-wing as they get older, with heavy left majorities (especially for social democracy and green ideology) tipping into dwindling left minorities (again, liberal-dominated) around middle age.[3]

The left cannot rely on the hope that it—or any of its constituent groups—will imminently achieve hegemonic status within all or part of any population. Certainly in open, non-totalitarian societies, it has never been the case historically that the left has achieved unanimous support, even in a single demographic group, let alone the population overall. As seen from the example of political parties in electoral space, it is becoming rare for left organisations even to attain majorities. Instead, the left can increasingly only hope to secure either pluralities or more-or-less stable coalitions of minorities. At the same time, it is also becoming increasingly hard to know what it would mean conceptually for there to be a left hegemony, given that populations are becoming more diverse and less monolithic. At best, the left can now aim for a more-than-temporary alliance between several overlapping left-leaning groups.

The left also cannot expect the majority to simply fall in line behind any minority—especially not one committed to radically overturning the *status quo*. Of course, this applies both to different ideological tendencies within the left as well as to the relations between the left and non-left (centre, right) within the wider population. If the left tries to bring this about artificially, this would utterly sacrifice all of its core concerns and values. It would be simply caving into the logic of oppression, hierarchy, discrimination, and competition—merely exchanging the places of its current victims and perpetrators. And it would bring society no closer to realising equality, justice, freedom, etc., as the left conceive of them. Meanwhile, if the left tries to simply wait for its hegemony to come about 'naturally', it may be waiting for a while, ultimately in vain. And by their very nature—i.e., by virtue of the fact that they cause suffering and damage to 'those without'—the problems the left feels called to address do not brook such excessive *attentisme*.

For the left, a blanket disposition of *impossibilism* and *rejectionism* is the fast-track to permanent defeat, minority, and opposition. If it refuses at least to make an effort to pursue opportunities to cooperate—even if there is the scope for cooperation with potential willing partners elsewhere on the left, in the centre, or on the right—this can lead to the paradoxical situation where the left cedes representation of one or more of its core principles to non-left groups and organisations. Aside from the sheer hypocrisy of refusing to even countenance cooperation, doing so is also strategically dangerous. Rejection by an intransigent left will simply drive rejected cooperation partners towards each other, often into more ideologically proximate and convenient partnerships. These may not only cost the left its input into the future trajectory of society—they may also be turned consciously and deliberately against the left and its activities and goals. This is not to say that the left has the duty to operate a blanket disposition of engagement either, especially not towards people and ideologies who are clearly determined to treat it as itself 'impossible' or worthy only of rejection. Rather, it should simply be prepared to offer and receive the hand of friendship and cooperation *where this looks like it might bear fruit.*

In other words, the left must always hold open the possibility of *possibilism.* Yet it must also recognise the inevitable costs this will have for how far it can pursue its aims. Cooperation will almost certainly reveal differences of interpretation regarding its concerns and values, and lead to their differential implementation in policy and strategy. But it can also carry the risk of their dilution or outright rejection. Different groups seek to 'decontest'—permanently and exclusively define—the meanings and implications of core terms in left analysis (e.g., power, structures, freedom, justice, etc.). How they do so will essentially determine how far cooperation between them means they have to give up different aspects of how they choose to interpret these terms. The left needs to be clear whether, and how far, it is prepared to sacrifice the monolithic homogeneity of its programme or the integrity of its principles to achieve—or reinforce—a popular majority and position of social strength.

The left's emphasis on cooperation is also framed and oriented by a very particular understanding of its values. Cooperation is essentially unworkable without at least a large measure of equality between the participating sides. The idea of partnership sends a signal that every group of 'those without' should suspend any attempts or claims to secure greater standing for themselves and their interests, in favour of allowing others in the same situation to have a similar say in formulating joint projects. Likewise, cooperation is one of the most effective mechanisms to ensure a just relationship between the various participants. It builds on the idea that to treat all sides fairly, common activities need to be planned in a way that allows 'those without' to derive both their rightful and adequate benefit from them. And cooperation is very clearly an expression, however circumscribed, of solidarity between its participants. It is predicated on the assumption that 'those without' and their allies need each other's support to bring about social outcomes they could not achieve by themselves, and offers a way of formalising the bonds of reciprocity between them.

At the same time, the left's values commit it to being open to new ideas and opportunities, and to exploring new avenues and approaches. In the first instance, cooperation across ideological lines is a way to intellectually free 'those without' and their fellow fighters. By cooperating, the left avoids its worldview becoming too entrenched and ossified, from becoming trapped by dogmatism. It is highly liberating to set aside prior ideological attachments, and embrace seeing concerns and values from a new perspective. Cooperation is also a consummate way to demonstrate and implement pluralism among 'those without' and their allies. It is about more than simply passively accepting the coexistence of multiple ideological positions on the left, as a mere inconvenient fact of complex society. Rather, it is a way of acknowledging them all as sources of worthwhile social insight, and actively exploring cross-fertilisation between established left outlooks.

Above all, cooperation bolsters the prospects of bringing about the progressive changes that 'those without' in society demand and require. It is a way for the left to open up new potential routes to achieving its goals—or, at least, to avoid closing off existing ones from the outset. The purity of the left's principled commitments cannot stand in the way of fostering and steering clear societal transformations. Exchange and collaboration between leftists with different outlooks on the left's concerns and values can spark unforeseen innovations, and the left as a movement should embrace the *de facto* radicalism of blending its current approaches to policy and strategy with injections of new ideological material. Put another way, the new opportunities that cooperation provides can offer the left ways out of its ideological impasses.

In general, again depending on what is at stake in any given situation, the left must remember that any part of it may have a vital contribution to make to the issue at hand. The left's penetration into every part of increasingly complex society creates fertile opportunities for its various strands' activities to shed new light on its concerns and values. Its presences in various domains of society and its engagement with various dimensions of personal identity lead to a nuanced, sophisticated interplay between many different 'left' angles on the movement's social priorities. The left's different parts learn from each other's ideas and practices, and such moments of cross-fertilisation between different left groups and their agents have been key to achieving some of the left movement's most momentous breakthroughs. For instance, there is a long and proud tradition for anti-colonial freedom movements to learn explicitly from one another's more or less successful experiences—Latin America, Ireland, Spain, the Balkans, India, the Middle East, Africa—which creates a kind of solidarity between them over time. Their tactics, violent or otherwise, have also been taken up by some of the most famous progressive social movements in history, from the suffragettes and the antifascists of the early 20th century to the anti-war and alter-globalisation protests a few decades later.

In every case, the decision of whether or not to cooperate touches on the choice left agents face between working within the norms of society as it is and prefiguring the norms of the society the left hopes to see. Certainly, the left's aim is a society built on a foundation of cooperation among all people (alongside their empowerment, parity between them, and their recognition as well). But in society as it now stands, this can only happen on the basis of 'good faith' reciprocity from others: people (not always on the left) who signal their honest willingness to share control, pool resources, exchange ideas, etc. Such 'good faith' is almost certainly easier to achieve contingently and incrementally for isolated moments of collaboration than as a blanket position. The left must be constantly sensitive to the cooperative opportunities every situation affords—as well as where they are lacking.

At the same time, the left needs to become far less piecemeal about cooperation. At the moment, left cooperation has a tendency to be somewhat patchy and asymmetric. The left's representative agents and organisations have a habit of relying on a familiar network or patterned arrangement of bodies and their various activities. This takes the form of a more-or-less formalised division of activist labour: for each grouping within the left, some representative agents and organisations take the lead in engineering spaces and opportunities for ideological encounters, while others follow along more passively. Some are more independent and autonomous in their activity on behalf of left concerns and values, others are more open to fostering collaborative links. At the moment, however, organisations like thinktanks, charities, or party-political foundations do much of the heavy lifting in creating opportunities for overlap and exchange, and showing routes to achieving policy changes.

In order to better reflect their shared commitments as part of the left movement, left groups need to instruct their agents to engage more frequently and evenly across organisational divides. The left needs to convert the one-sided, unidirectional 'leader-follower' relations between different categories of agents and organisations into reciprocal, multidirectional relations of collaborative sharing, pooling, exchange, and support. Of course, such a reform of the left's own internal dynamics is a central part of downplaying the dominance of particular well-established organisations (parties, unions, etc.) at the expense of newer ones. But more fundamentally, it also increases the left's ability to keep paying attention to all its chosen concerns, values, dimensions of identity, and societal domains to a relatively equivalent degree.

Concrete instances of cooperation will always have to be guided by the requirements imposed and opportunities afforded by the particular situations in which they take place. However, the urgency of the issues the left must confront means that it is often not enough simply to wait for *ad hoc*, spontaneous cooperation to emerge between agents and organisations. To avoid potentially costly delays and hesitation, the left needs to create systematic cooperation frameworks that left agents and organisations can appeal to. The purpose of these would be to foster and underpin projects of reciprocal control-sharing, resource-pooling, exchanges of ideas, and formulation of common rules for left activism across the dimensions of personal identity and societal domains. Such frameworks would allow left activists to share their particular experiences of fighting for 'those without' in specific situations with the left movement at large, and lay the policy and strategic groundwork for cooperation.

The left's current approach of having particular organisations tasked with bringing together others imposes an unfair burden on them. In reality, all left agents and organisations should be searching proactively for opportunities to cooperate across the movement, irrespective of the ideological divisions between them. Instead, the left needs an overarching body that brings together and harmonises the policy-research and strategy-development functions of left organisations across the movement. Avoiding both intellectual and practical 'siloisation' or 'Balkanisation' requires every left group to make conscious efforts to bridge the divides between them. Only by actively seeking out ways to overcome and replace competitive tendencies within the left will the movement become capable of developing ways for its organised agents to jointly increase their majority support and improve their position of strength within the population.

## NOTES

1. Simone Abendschön and Stephanie Steinmetz, 'Women's Party Preferences in a European Context', *Social Politics* 21(2) (2014), 315-44; Ronald Inglehart and Pippa Norris, 'The developmental theory of the gender gap: women's and men's voting behavior in global perspective', *International Political Science Review* 21(4) (2000), 441-63; Niels Spierings and Andrej Zaslove, 'Gender, populist attitudes, and voting: explaining the gender gap in voting for populist radical right and populist radical left parties', *West European Politics* 40(4) (2017), 821-47.

2. Giedo Jansen, Geoffrey Evans, and Nan Dirk de Graaf, 'Class voting and Left-Right party positions: A comparative study of 15 Western democracies, 1960-2005', *Social Science Research* 42(2) (2013), 376-400; Oddbjørn Knutsen, *Class Voting in Western Europe: A Comparative Longitudinal Study* (Lanham, MD: Lexington Books, 2006).

3. Ron Johnston, Kelvyn Jones, and David Manley, 'Age, sex, qualification and voting at recent English general elections: an alternative exploratory approach', *Electoral Studies* 51(1) (2018), 24-37; Warren E. Miller, 'Generational Changes and Party Identification', *Political Behavior* 14(3) (1992), 333-52; James Tilley and Geoffrey Evans, 'Ageing and generational effects on vote choice: combining cross-sectional and panel data to estimate APC effects', *Electoral Studies* 33(1) (2014), 19-27.

# METHODS OF COOPERATION

If cooperation is such a vital way for the left to advance its principles and goals, then who should it be seeking to work with, and to what ends? First and foremost, left groups must start by recognising that no single one of them automatically holds the answers to all social problems, even those it has taken the lead on flagging as social concerns. Similarly, no left group can claim to have exclusive 'ownership' of any given value, in the sense of having its only correct interpretation and acting as its only true advocate. No group in the population has a monopoly on experiencing oppression, hierarchy, discrimination, or competition, and none can claim to have the only valid criticisms of inequality, injustice, lack of solidarity, unfreedom, monism, and absence of progress. One of the most self-aware moves any left group can make, therefore, is knowing when it needs others to help widen its gaze.

This does not necessarily just apply within the left either. Of course, for anyone on the left, being a committed co-member of a movement that is predicated on being willing to fight for 'those without' is an obvious signal that someone would make a potential partner for cooperation. But this willingness does not necessarily end abruptly at the boundaries of the left. There are both social concerns and values where the left has room for overlap—and hence room to engage—with groups in the centre and on the right as well. Ideological innovation and cross-fertilisation does not ever truly respect the largely artificial divides imposed on it by the activists engaged in ideological contests. Left ideologies of all stripes have a long tradition of appropriating and repurposing ideas and practices from their neighbours, even their most existential enemies. The reappropriation of European imperial, chauvinist understandings of nationalism by movements who were fighting to oppose and liberate their territories from European colonialism is a particularly powerful example.[1] Cooperation across the ideological spectrum is thus not necessarily a betrayal of left principles, but can be a way to assert and further them within society—so long as they are not warped beyond recognition in the process.

It is worth dispelling some areas of confusion about what cooperation requires of left groups and agents that pursue it. First, cooperation does not necessarily equate to *moderation*, which describes a strategy of deliberate self-limitation in both ideas and practices. At the level of identifying concerns and formulating values, it means avoiding extreme, unusual, or rigidly dogmatic interpretations—steering consciously towards intermediate, standard positions resembling those already accepted by other sides who might act as potential partners. This ideological averageness or mediocrity is reflected in a tempering of the manner in which we seek to address our concerns and realise our values. Violent or excessively unrestrained means are ruled out in favour of milder, gentler approaches, with a more modest horizon of expectation for the extent of societal changes we will achieve.

By contrast, cooperation does not need to involve any self-limitation in ideas or practices. Rather, it can be a way for would-be cooperating partners to overcome constraints that the prevailing social context places on them, by supporting principles and enabling strategies they could not hope to pursue purely by themselves. It is entirely possible to have a radical transformative vision for society alongside a clear sense of the incremental pragmatic steps that would be required to realise it. It can be based on ideas that are not only rigorous and detailed, but highly innovative, even outstandingly unique relative to the others on offer in that context. It does not mean ruling out any of the available means, but can be designed specifically to mobilise ones that derive from intensely visceral judgments on society, which can include jointly-planned violent challenges to the *status quo*. Lastly, cooperation does not need to be for limited purposes, but can be exactly what the left needs to help bring about a more ambitious transformation of society than would otherwise be possible.

Second, cooperation does not have to mean *compromise*, which refers to a strategy of tit-for-tat trading-off of ideas and practices with a would-be partner to achieve select aspects of (mutually rival) social visions. At its core lies an assumption that social concerns and values are bargaining chips, to be played and—crucially— prejudicially conceded at whim as part of the negotiation process. Finding a way between the various sides' starting 'bids' is thus a matter of partial mutual surrender. We must be prepared to weaken or even abandon our principles and goals to reach a conclusion that everyone can commit to. In turn, this compromise conclusion is by definition an incompletely satisfying second-best, a derogatory and even objectionable sacrifice made in exchange for at least some ideological gain. Compromise is framed as a deal to settle differences between the various participating sides, which is sometimes reached through outside arbitration, and always (at least implicitly, and however reluctantly) endorsed by the consent of all sides.

Cooperation is subtly different, as it focuses on partners working together to achieve a partial (but fully shared) social vision. It does not automatically need all social concerns and values to be at stake. Co-operating partners can join forces on specific concerns, or help each other in realising certain values, without touching on any of the others. Left cooperation is not a 'way between' but a 'way that combines' different sides' starting bids—precisely where, and insofar as, overlaps on addressing oppression, hierarchy, etc., or realising equality, justice, etc., already exist. We can commit to a general direction that still leaves room for divergence on details, and we can agree a consensus on key priorities that are prerequisites for—but also compatible with—several options for continuation further down the line. Left cooperation takes satisfaction from the fact that some mutually-sought-after progress is made, rather than resenting the fact that some of its principles and goals were left aside in the process. It does not even require participants to settle their differences, as it can happen even when these differences have only been tactically suspended so as to achieve defined joint purposes.

Third, cooperation does not always have to lead to *elision*, or a permanent and comprehensive fusion, between the people that undertake it. This is unification in an extremely literal sense, based on blurring and ultimately eroding not just the ideological but also the social discreteness of previously distinct sets of people. It is not the smoothing-over of differences in principles and goals that is the end of elision; rather, these are an instrumental stage towards a wholesale eradication of the boundaries between social groups. In part, this represents a deliberate loss of the different sides' ideological character, as the process of elision 'decouples' people and groups from their previous positions on the ideological spectrum. In this respect, elision is the ultimate denial of ideological contestation. The ideological perspectives of the eliding groups are simply conflated, and any previous differences of emphasis or interpretation over concerns and values either reconciled or omitted from future discussion. Elision is thus a highly anti-pluralist move, as it destroys the social foundations of ideological difference in order to reinforce a single new hegemonic position.

Instead, cooperation is more narrowly defined as engaging with others on specific contingent issues, with no necessary link to any deeper or more lasting unification. Its aim is merely to offer a counterpoint to competitive behaviour, based on hostility, enmity, even destructive one-upmanship. Left cooperation does not require the erosion of ideological or social boundaries between its participants—in fact, it depends almost by definition on different sides engaging reciprocally and supportively with one another *despite* still remaining separate. These sides also retain their discrete ideological characters, within and outside the left movement, since the point of cooperation is to find areas where they are prepared to bridge and overcome differences in how they conceive of social concerns and values. Cooperation does not then, as such, deny that there will be ideological contestation between the sides participating in it—and it does not necessarily expect that their ideological perspectives will be reconciled in other areas. Left cooperation, in other words, is entirely pluralistic, as it aims for ideological overlap without aspiring to a new hegemony.

For each left group and its representative agents and organisations, there is essentially a series of concentric circles of potential cooperation partners, working outwards from their own ideological position. Which other groups lie within each of these circles can vary significantly from one situation to the next, and depends fundamentally on how the group at the epicentre ranks its social concerns, conceives of its values, reflects personal identities, and operates in different societal domains. Each group must be acutely aware of where its own constellation of rankings, conceptions, etc., sits on the ideological spectrum compared to those of other groups who also engage with the social issues raised in each situation. This is a vital prerequisite to determining how deep a range of shared principles can be used as the basis for cooperation—and how far cooperation between them is possible at all.

Identifying which other groups might be more or less ideologically suited for cooperation does not necessarily make someone either a 'centrist' or an 'extremist'. These circles can radiate outwards in any relative direction along the spectrum of available ideological perspectives. The ideological position of left cooperation depends entirely on who the left happens to be cooperating with. Depending on the issue at hand, they may be left-left, left-centre, or even at times cut across the prevailing left-right spectrum entirely—as with, for instance, the nationalisation of strategic industries, electoral reform, or anti-corruption laws respectively. All that this requires is that groups and their agents know their own relative position within ideological space. They need to know where they fit within the overall distribution of concerns and values among the population as a whole, and within 'their' immediate wing of the spectrum as its own social ecosystem. In spatial or anthropological terms, they need to be aware of their ideological *neighbourhood*, to the extent of recognising the extent to which they share *kinship* with other groups and their agents.

For the left, this means that cooperation starts within the left, but can move beyond it and across to the centre and right if necessary (and possible) too. Certainly, left groups have a closer initial affinity with other left groups, since they share similar principles and goals—even if they differ in the specifics of policy and strategy. This affinity becomes weaker the further one moves across the spectrum, as centrist and right groups depart ever more from the left's concerns and values. Yet there are clear situations where left-only cooperation fails or is not enough, usually because left groups prove unsuccessful in overcoming their ideological divisions, or even together are unable to secure majority popular support or establish a position of sufficient strength. In these cases, the most common outcome is some form of centre-left cooperation—such as with now increasingly common 'traffic light' parliamentary coalitions between social democrats, liberals, and greens, or the cooption of middle-class radicals and democrats in revolutions spearheaded by the socialist working class. But it can occasionally lead to contingent, time-limited *rapprochements* between left and right as well—as in 'grand coalitions' between social democrats and Christian democrats, or the historical alignments between conservative aristocrats and the socialist working class to limit the excesses of emergent liberal capitalism.

Here, it is important to remember that groups and their agents—and movements as a whole—often overlap on the ideological spectrum. In their ongoing contests over social concerns and values, they are as much trying to occupy the same ideological space as they are cornering off their 'own' separate space for themselves. This has both positive and negative effects on the prospects for cooperation between them. On the positive side, it makes it appreciably easier to find a basis for shared cooperative programmes that can help social groups aggregate their shares of popular support and combine their strengths. However, on the negative side, if the same groups prefer to compete rather than cooperate, this ideological overlap also allows them to threaten or attempt to 'steal' popular support from one another, and undermine each other's strengths. This bivalence means that areas of ideological overlap between social groups lay the basic groundwork for both mutual inclusion and exclusion between them—for both sharing and conflicting over their 'ownership' of concerns and values.

This means that every left group and its agents must have a very clear idea of who is a 'yes', a 'maybe', and a 'no' for them as potential cooperation partners on every issue important to them. To decide this, what is needed as well as an accurate assessment of the balance of social forces is a clear categorisation of all of them in terms of their preparedness to collaborate with the left—ranging from open to amenable to averse to cooperation. In some cases, this may be a blanket judgment—as with categorically opposing 'far-right' ideologies that are explicitly and unapologetically committed to antisemitic, Islamophobic, misogynistic, or white-supremacist positions. In others, it may vary depending on the issues or situations in question—such as conservatives on questions of environmental protections, Christian democrats on family welfare provision, or libertarians on opposing privacy infringements by societal surveillance. Overall, the left must explicitly acknowledge that there are some groups in contemporary society with whom cooperation is viable, even desirable, and others with whom it is impossible, or deeply unwise. Although the left should certainly hold open the possibility of collaboration with the centre and the right, it must also recognise that this is ultimately less likely than mutual enmity.

Yet the left cannot simply crush those with whom it cannot cooperate, either in the centre or on the right. This would be a straightforward inversion of the left's social concerns: oppressing the previously empowered, subordinating erstwhile hierarchical leaders, discriminating against those who were formerly recognised, and ensuring that prior winners of competition are now its losers. It would also come no nearer to realising the left's values, but simply rearrange the distribution of costs and benefits under the present regime of inequality, injustice, partial freedom, etc. It is an open question whether that is a societal state that actually achieves the left's goals. It may doubtless be temporarily satisfying as a way of asserting the position of 'those without'. But in the end, the left needs to go beyond that to secure full eventual buy-in from all 'those with' and all 'those without', regardless of their current left-right leanings.

Instead, the left should operate a strategy of 'cooperation or cooption'. It must learn to use areas of ideological overlap on concerns and values to make overtures to groups who are prepared to cooperate, and at the same time to 'outbid' and outmanoeuvre those who are not willing to do so to starve them of popular support and capacity for social action. At the heart of this strategy must lie the construction of a '*left bloc*' or '*left front*'. This, simply put, is the idea of an agreement between otherwise mutually independent and potentially rivalrous left groups to form a single 'side' for the purposes of ideological contests. It takes the form of a systematic cooperation arrangement reached through a conscious alliance, rather than merely a situation of coincidental alignment reached accidentally through separate paths of policy reasoning. In order to achieve majority-upwards levels of support in the population, this 'left bloc' can also be expanded to include elements from beyond the left (centre, right) who are willing to cooperate—converting the 'left front' into a 'popular front'.

Like other forms of cooperation, this bloc or front does not need to be a blanket arrangement, but can be established in a more contingent way. It can be time-limited, such as for the duration of an election period, or parliamentary term, or for the time it takes to see certain policies through their implementation processes. The front can also be limited in its geographical extent, operating exclusively at the level of local authorities, regional or state governments, or at the national as opposed to the supranational/international tier. Or it can be formed on specific issues, or for certain delimited purposes, such as achieving or preventing particular outcomes—changes in public policy, legislation, or cultural norms—and supporting or resisting certain people—significant figures from government, business, the church, academia, the media, etc.

The depth and durability of this front ultimately comes down to how prepared left groups are to exchange the purity (homogeneity and integrity) of their ideological principles for the completeness (efficacious achievement) of their ideological goals. As the bodies who lead the combined activist efforts of such a front, it is up to each left organisation and its constituent agents to have a clear sense of their own prioritisation of the principles they are bound to represent. This is not as such a question of the unique constellation of emphases between concerns and values, and the orientation towards dimensions and domains they are imbued with by 'their' left groups. Rather, it is a matter of the order in which these concerns, values, etc., can be deprioritised—or, as a second best, diluted or entirely sacrificed—in the process of negotiating an ideological front.

In other words, left organisations must have a clear sense of which parts of their ideological 'wishlist' are non-negotiable 'red lines' when they seek out opportunities for cooperation. Each left group must know which issues it wants its agents to lead on, and where it is willing for them to collaborate; which they need to adhere to, and where it is prepared for them to soften their stance. Ultimately, this comes down to determining how much of its independent ideological identity each left group is prepared to maintain or give up—and, relatedly, how much independent agency it wants to leave its representatives. Out of the myriad separate prioritising decisions by the many would-be members of a left front emerges the skeleton basis on which this front can emerge—not just in terms of its underlying principles and eventual goals, but also as a guide to its activities.

In this respect, it is the responsibility of each of the left's intersecting constitutive groups to consider how it will position itself towards the prospect of forming a left front. Such a front cannot be achieved by simply introducing steering bodies at the level of the left movement as a whole. That is not the organic, situation- and issue-driven basis on which any left cooperation should emerge, and runs completely counter to the left's approach to social power and social structures. Rather, every part of the left needs to pre-empt the initial exploratory stages of cooperation negotiations by transparently signalling its intentions and preferences. Doing so would encourage left groups and their representative organisations to become more self-aware and clearer about their ideological position within the left and within society at large.

The aim of this is to enable left organisations to better calculate which parts of their programme stand a good chance of being successfully passed and implemented within society as it stands. It would also allow them to identify in advance the preferred partners with whom they would cooperate to make this happen, and begin the process of agitating for popular support and a stronger social position. The left needs to recall that its programmes are ultimately not just designed for itself as a movement, but for society as a whole. Their major role is to motivate the acceptance of left concerns and adoption of left values across the population, even well beyond the left—and it is by that criterion that the left's cooperative efforts should be judged.

## NOTE

1. Adria K. Lawrence, *Imperial rule and the politics of nationalism: Anti-colonial protest in the French Empire* (Cambridge: Cambridge University Press, 2013); John M. Lonsdale, 'Anti-Colonial Nationalism and Patriotism in Sub-Saharan Africa', in John Breuilly (ed.), *The Oxford Handbook of the History of Nationalism* (Oxford: Oxford University Press, 2013); Erez Manela, *The Wilsonian Moment: Self-Determination and the International Origins of Anticolonial Nationalism* (Oxford: Oxford University Press, 2009).

# III

# Left strategy

# PAST AND FUTURE

As a progressive movement, the left is committed to a belief in both the capacity and the need for the future to improve on the present and the past. But what is the precise relationship between the past and the future? Every social ideology stands in the same reciprocal relationship towards society and the way it changes over time. On the one hand, it always tries to respond to such changes, and make the most of the opportunities they present to further its social aims. On the other hand, it also tries to steer them, to either exacerbate or mitigate their impacts on both the most and the least privileged and advantaged in society. What makes the progressive left stand out is its particular focus on the future. In the way in which it deals with societal changes, the left prioritises where their effects will lead, and tries to ascertain, even predict, the course of causal chains that lead to them.

To do this, the left needs a clear sense of what it thinks the past, present, future are. It also needs an understanding of how they are connected to each other, in particular the historical trajectory that binds them into a specific sequence or succession. First, the left sees past, present, and future as characterised by discontinuity and difference rather than continuity and identity. For progressives, the periodisation and shifts of past-present-future are a question of discreteness and change—i.e., they conceive of history *as* a trajectory in the first place, embracing a dynamic view of society rather than the static conception adopted by (some) reactionary ideologies. Second, the progressive left focuses on how the present and future build on the past, in contrast to (other) reactionaries who see the present and future as detracting from it. In general, progressives see time's arrow as not just moving forward (as a baseline), but also (at least able to be turned) upward—as opposed to the (baseline, able to be turned) downward reactionary logic of 'decline and fall'.[1]

The left's commitment to progress as a discrete social value has both diagnostic and critical/positive elements. On the diagnostic side, being progressive means being self-aware. It requires us to know where we think society lies on its historical trajectory, and be able to situate our momentary context in the grander scheme of society's evolution. It also means knowing where we fit into this trajectory, and how we relate to our own context given our ideological commitments. This self-awareness is not necessarily premised on a detailed conception of what the future will look like. Rather, it is more based on an understanding of how far society has come from the past to the present, and in what ways precisely it has developed, coupled with a capacity to project these developments forward in a more than vaguely speculative way.

On the critical/positive side, being progressive also means being optimistic. It implies that the left has both the aspiration and expectation that its responses to deep societal changes, and its attempts to steer them, will (on balance) be more successful than not in addressing its concerns and realising its values. It means that moving forward, or improving, is premised on overcoming the past and present—i.e., the progressiveness of the future is decided by its specific divergence from past and present, and is thus defined in terms of both of them. Progressive optimism is not, as such, rooted in a general condemnation or dismissal of society's past. Instead, it merely reflects an in-built view that the past and present are imperfect, and an expectation that the passage of time will only reveal their flaws more clearly—and implicitly make clear the 'right' trajectory for the future.

Together, this puts the left into a somewhat ambiguous relationship with the past. On the one hand, it means that the left must be attentive to and learn from the past. Left groups and organisations not only must not ignore the past, but actively need to seek out information about it to guide their approach to contemporary social concerns. Addressing the left's social concerns is not just about avoiding some abstract negative ways in which power, societal structures, attitudes, or behaviour could theoretically impact 'those without' in society. Doing so is specifically designed to end, overcome, and redress the concrete negative experiences that the disadvantaged and underprivileged have had up to that point.[2] Left ideology is not in the business of inventing social evils that have no basis in reality. Rather, it is the evils that exist and have existed previously that create the need for a left response.

In other words, a vital part of how the left devises principles and goals for how to empower 'those without' and their allies, bring about greater parity between them, grant them greater recognition, and foster cooperation among them is by looking carefully at how these aims were neglected historically. The left responds explicitly to past abuses of power: labour exploitation, marital subjugation, denials of rights, or terrorism and violence. It seeks to undo the toxic uses to which social structures have previously been put: the creation of enslaved and dehumanised 'underclasses', self-reinforcing and self-perpetuating elites, and authoritarian or totalitarian dictatorship. The left fights to end the vicious, vile way in which society has treated certain groups for many long years: religious and ethnic persecution, the 'unnaturalisation' of 'deviant' sexual and gender identities and behaviours, or female sexualisation and objectification. And it aims to repair the devastation that past hostilities have left in their wake: mass-destructive total warfare, near-irreconcilable mistrust between social groups, or genocide and other crimes against humanity.

At the same time, on the other hand, the past also cannot be allowed to stand in the way of the future. Certainly, the past (and its legacy in the present) is the main motive reason for the left to undertake progressive change in society. But equally, by the same token, it is also only the starting-point for social development. The future the left has in view must concede to the past and present insofar as they frame the initial conditions in which the left must operate when it tries to steer societal changes in its preferred direction. They partly determine what counts as a viable or impossible change, and as modest or ambitious progress, for the context and the people in question. Yet ultimately, the point of progress is to depart from the past: to free itself from its constraints, and draw a line under its effects. The left must be attentive, and open, to the idea that for every social evil it sets out to address, there comes a point when, for all intents and purposes, it has finally been completely overcome. In other words, the left must know when it needs to move on from the past.

The left has to recognise that the past is settled—in fact, if not in evaluation. Of course, facts do not 'speak for themselves', and debating the significance of the past (its interpretation, moral verdict, etc.) does partly determine the left's views about the present and future. But this is always done with a view turned away from the past. The past itself is not actually at stake in these debates, because it cannot fundamentally be changed—rather, it is the past's reception, its narrative framing, its ideological deployment that are at issue in later analysis. By contrast, much of the future is still yet to be determined. The past and present may impose some legacy constraints on the future, but these do not have a wholly unlimited reach or duration. In other words, the future is ultimately still entirely changeable—and the left has to remember that there is far more at stake in determining the direction of the future than in determining the interpretation of the past.

Ideologically, this means that the left needs to acknowledge a temporal tension within the way it adheres to certain social concerns (in varying emphases) and certain values (in varying conceptualisations). On the one hand, they are inherent to what it means to be 'left'. In *some* way, shape, or form, they are always going to be present, as the left must cleave to a certain outlook and principles consistently in order to maintain its essential ideological integrity. On the other hand, they are products of—and refer to—a very particular set of contextual circumstances, points not just in space but also in time.[3] In the *precise* way, shape, or form they assume at any given time, they are similarly always going to be contingent, and the left must hold open the possibility that they will subsequently change in ways that are not entirely predictable. The difference between the two may be one of definition and interpretation, or of prioritisation. This gives the left an extremely precarious balancing act to perform. Crucially, it needs to take great care in sustaining at the same time its vision of what is, or should be, right or necessary 'transcontextually'—i.e., across and irrespective of differences in space and time—as well as a recognition of what is (or is seen as) right or necessary in a given momentary context. Compared to each other, how the left would like to address its concerns and realise its values ideally, in general, or in the long run, may far outstrip what society can 'take' at any given point. This is the motivating tension behind debates, for instance, about setting gradual versus ambitious targets for achieving gender parity in government cabinets, company boards, academic faculties, or about mediating claims for tolerance from religious minorities and LGBTQ* groups in contexts where homophobia and transphobia are still often given faith-based justifications.

The left's societal vision can be highly aspirational; its recognition may well be dully concessive. Not every change can be immediate; not every issue can be perfectly resolved. This does not by any means invalidate its concerns and values. It also does not indicate that either the left's vision or its contextual recognition are ideologically defective—the former by being 'detached from reality', the latter through too much deviation or sacrifice of principle. But the left does need to accept that despite these differences between inherent and contextual manifestations of its ideology, the two must always be linked together into a coherent programme at every point in space and time—which means that it must engage in a constant process of self-reevaluation.

This becomes most acutely relevant in the case of past controversies, debates, and disputes within the left as a movement. Left history is full of severe disagreements between different left groups as to the 'correct' way to address specific social concerns and interpret certain values, or the 'right' relative emphasis to be placed on particular dimensions of identity and societal domains. One of the most internecine left disputes has been over how extensively equality should be defined, with liberals tending to err on the side of equal rights of citizenship, and socialists preferring comprehensive equal distributions of material resources. Similarly, the concept of 'intersectionality' itself stems from the clear dissatisfaction felt by lower-income women of colour that their experiences of underprivilege and disadvantage tended to be written out of narratives of classism (white-centric and male-centric), sexism (middle-class and white-centric), and racism (male-centric).[4] The result has often been conscious mutual divergence—even aversion—between the left groups concerned.

In reality, it does not matter what originally motivated any given divergence. It can be the result of a conflict between sincerely-held views, it may be cynical or calculated, or it could be down to differences in groups' preparedness to compromise (purism vs dilution, etc.). The key point is that left-left divergences are qualitatively different from the left's clashes with the centre and the right. They stem from differences *more of degree than kind* over how to remedy the past and shape the future. Moreover, the left needs to recognise that all such divergences are specific to the contexts in which they happened. They do not necessarily have any more to say about the underlying or inherent 'leftness' of any of the groups concerned, at least not beyond (i.e., before and after) these contexts themselves. Rhetoric of 'never trusting' a given ideology and its exponents again in the wake of a particular crisis within the left movement—ranging from supporting wars to curbing welfare programmes—miss the point that ideologies are not static, but in a constant state of evolution and self-overcoming. It is not their 'leftness' that changes, but the way in which it manifests from context to context.

This means that the left needs to both acknowledge and learn from past disputes *and* consciously move on from them, and not let past disagreement block future cooperative work. On the one hand, it is extremely important to ensure that the left does not repeat any mistakes in cases of future disputes. It cannot pretend that they did not happen, as ignoring them merely risks them reemerging later in different guises, allowing them to fester as potential points of left disunity. On the other hand, it is vital for the left to accept that past disputes are done—they are over, their time lies in the past. They cannot be undone by constantly relitigating them well beyond their original context, as doing so only risks introducing them into every other conceivable future conflict, entrenching them as sources of left division. The first approach suppresses disputes rather than resolving them; the second reanimates disputes instead of overcoming them.

The left especially needs to avoid letting issue-specific disputes (over individual concerns, values, etc.) escalate into existential disputes among left factions. These are a peculiarly toxic instance of the conflictual possibilities of ideological overlap, whereby each participant in the dispute seeks to claim exclusive 'ownership' over left identity, and deny the 'left-ness' of other left groups. Such an ideological extrapolation is self-evidently analytically incorrect. Simply disagreeing over whether, or how, to fight for 'those without' in a specific situation does not necessarily reveal anything about either side's willingness to do so in other situations, or as a general commitment. But more pressingly, it is outstandingly strategically unhelpful to assume that it does. That loses sight of the relevant area of dispute, blurs together issues and contexts in a way that undermines effective left activism, and makes left-on-left conflict needlessly spill over beyond, and outlast, its contingent appearance.

Here, it is important for left to remember that its programme consists of themes (principles, goals, policies, strategies) that are interrelated, but which do not have to stand or fall as a monolithic unity. As outlined earlier, it is entirely possible to have issue-specific as well as *en bloc* cooperation. The left cannot let unrelated or mutu- ally irrelevant issues and disputes stand in the way of cooperation on other particular questions—there is too much at stake for the left to force an 'all or nothing' choice between homogeneity and fragmentation. Issue-specific flexibility is both an opportunity and a necessity. It allows the left to 'hive off' disputes into 'smaller-scale' areas of non-cooperation, in the interests of insulating wider left cooperation from metastasising corrosive effects. Or it lets the left find 'smaller-scale' areas of cooperation to gradually build trust, from which to expand and overcome wider left non-cooperation.

Part of fostering left self-reevaluation, and recognising the tension between inherent and contextual approaches to concerns and commitments to values, is abandoning the logic of 'being on the right/ wrong side of history'. First, just as the left does not have a monopoly on solving social problems, it must recognise that it also does not have a monopoly on defining or predicting the trajectory of history. This trajectory is the result of human agency being superimposed onto deep changes in the underlying character of society. Obviously, the left and its agents and organisations are not the only social force attempting to exercise their agency in this way. Even with the best will to cooperate, the left will always find itself competing against the centre and right in its response to these changes, and its attempts to steer them in the 'correct' direction.

Second, the left must always bear in mind the gap between societal change and societal progress. Change is something that many people are at least dimly aware of even as it is taking place. But as much as progress can be an aspiration that drives their reaction to this change, it is ultimately a retrospective evaluation. In the end, the logic of the 'right or wrong side of history' is about defending one's own past or present versus condemning others' past or present. It tends to be used in conjunction with narratives about the supposed trajectory of past-present-future to contextualise and legitimise, for instance, support for enfranchising women, under-18s, or foreign residents; equal rights to marriage and adoption for LGBTQ* people; or shifting to a 'world without work' in response to the rise of automation in production. Instead, the left's real focus should be on trying to 'get the future right'. There is no guarantee that any part of the left is even best placed to know how best to bring about the changes it would retrospectively regard as progressive. This is why its strategy must always have the scope for cooperation beyond its ideological borders.

The left should abandon the logic of resentment, grudge-holding, and hanging onto residual enmity or hostility. Instead, it should acknowledge the strategic importance of 'forgiving and forgetting'. There is no group or organisation that has a perfect record at translating its visions into every context. Redressing the past and shaping the future is an intrinsically uncertain activity, and no person or group deserves greater or lesser credit than any other for how well it has performed in doing so. If the left's members are to cooperate, they must be prepared to treat would-be partners with respectful consideration. They cannot hope to forge successful partnerships if they demand for themselves a standard of treatment they are not prepared to extend to others in return, or are prepared to offer them little more than half-hearted support. The left needs to draw a firm line to prevent their acknowledgment of others' ideological differences from hardening into a toxic factionalism, which warps open-minded tolerance into dogmatic condemnation.

To truly be able to move from the past to the future, the left needs mechanisms to systematise and regulate ideological disputes, both within the left movement and beyond its borders. The singular purpose of such mechanisms should be to resolve such disputes, or at least find settlements that can prevent their interminable continuation and constant re-emergence.[5] The left urgently needs processes in place to bring about reconciliation between left groups—especially between their representative agents and organisations, since they are *de facto* at the 'frontline' of efforts to cooperate strategically across group boundaries. The aim of this is to iron out a potential clash between two of the left's key values: stopping *pluralism* from entrenching as factionalism to the extent that it stands in the way of *progress*.

Although such mechanisms can be *ad hoc* and informal, the sheer frequency of ideological disputes suggests that a proper solution requires them to be institutionalised. Each left group needs permanent investigation, arbitration, and conciliation bodies to address disputes in which it is involved—either internally, or with other groups. Ideally, these should be attached to its already-existing representative organisations, and the rules for how they should carry out their investigation, arbitration, and conciliation functions appended to the terms by which these organisations are mandated by the groups in question. But some equivalent of these bodies also needs to exist for the left movement as a whole. As with the other proposals outlined earlier, the best way to realise this is through a federal network of such bodies with a vertical appeals system, along with meaningful disciplinary and enforcement mechanisms. In this way, institutionalising dispute resolution can help provide the clarity the left on relies to properly transcend the past and head open-minded into the future.

## NOTES

1. See, for instance, Michael Bentley, *Modern Historiography: An Introduction* (Abingdon: Routledge, 1999); Adam Budd (ed.), *The Modern Historiography Reader* (Abingdon: Routledge, 2009); Anna Green and Kathleen Troup, *The Houses of History: A Critical Reader in History and Theory* (Manchester: Manchester University Press, 2016).
2. Elazar Barkan, *The Guilt of Nations: Restitution and Negotiating Historical Injustices* (New York, NY: W.W. Norton & Co., 2000); Jeff Spinner-Halev, 'Historical Injustice', in David Estlund (ed.), *The Oxford Handbook of Political Philosophy* (Oxford: Oxford University Press, 2012), 319-35; Janna Thompson, *Taking Responsibility for the Past: Reparation and Historical Justice* (Cambridge: Polity, 2002).
3. Keith DeRose, *The Case for Contextualism: Knowledge, Skepticism, and Context* (Oxford: Oxford University Press, 2009); James Tully (ed.), *Meaning and Context: Quentin Skinner and His Critics* (Princeton, NJ: Princeton University Press, 1989).
4. Combahee River Collective, 'A Black Feminist Statement', in Zillah R. Eisenstein (ed.), *Capitalist Patriarchy and the Case for Socialist Feminism* (New York, NY: Monthly Review Press, 1978); bell hooks, *Ain't I A Woman* (London: Pluto Press, 1987); Keeanga-Yamahtta Taylor (ed.),

*How We Get Free: Black Feminism and the Combahee River Collective* (Chicago, IL: Haymarket Books, 2017).

5. Priscilla B. Hayner, *Unspeakable Truths: Facing Challenge of Truth Commissions* (Abingdon: Routledge, 2010); Robert Rotberg and Dennis Thompson (eds.). *Truth versus Justice: The Morality of Truth Commissions* (Princeton, NJ: Princeton University Press, 2000).

# PERSONALITY AND POLICY

How should the left address the role that major personalities play in ideological movements? The left's aims are fundamentally socially-oriented. Of course, it cares passionately about individual people—its goal, after all, is to improve the societal position of every member of the disadvantaged, the underprivileged, 'those without'. But it recognises that people derive their identity, meanings, purposes, capacities, etc., from the way in which they fit into society, and their position in relation to others within it. The left's concerns and values are designed to impose limits on *any single* individual's capacity to assert themselves *over* society, in exchange for maximising *all* individuals' capacity to assert themselves *within* it. Yet it is operating in a world where rival ideologies and movements are entirely comfortable with single individuals amassing a lot of concentrated power, and sitting at the centre of steeply towering hierarchies.

This sets a limit to how far the left can actually prefigure a situation where no single individual can dominate any part of society. But its ideological authenticity requires that it nevertheless try to do so as and where it can—and that this is best achieved by first prefiguring it within the left itself, to 'show the way' for the rest of society. Specifically, within and among the left's groups, agents, and organisations, no single person or any combination of people should seek to assert themselves over the left—either in part or as a whole. Rather, the left needs to foster all its members' abilities to assert themselves within the movement. Within left groups, this means that leftists need to demonstrate clearly that they value each other as co-fighters on the same ideological side of social struggles. This includes granting one another the space and respect to fully realise their own complex personal identities and pursue their engagements in different societal domains. In left organisations, this is formalised by giving all their constituent agents equal and extensive rights, and introducing inclusive, participatory approaches to answering questions of organisational policy and strategy.

After all, one of the left's most urgent aims is that none of the many representative left agents and organisations oriented towards different dimensions of personal identity or domains of society take on a dominant or preeminent role within the movement. The corollary of this is that every member of the left needs to be given complete internal, self-oriented autonomy and self-determination. They need to be given the freedom to carry out their chosen activities on behalf of the disadvantaged and underprivileged—and entrusted with the responsibility of devising their own methods of doing so if they choose. Of course, others can offer them support and assistance, but their capacity to act as left activists must not be made to depend conditionally on anyone else. They must be allowed to inform themselves, reflect on social issues, and come to ideological conclusions as they see fit. And other leftists must respect their decisions about which of their personal identities or societal engagements they choose to prioritise, and which to downplay, in their overall contribution to left activism.

This applies inclusively to all left groups and their representative agents. Whether in their self-constituted bodies or within the formal mandates of their organisations, leftists need to be allowed—and trusted—to direct their own affairs, exempt from control or coercion by others. Each left group needs to exercise unhindered decisive control over its membership, over the representative personnel it mandates to its organisations, and the internal regulations and structures by which its activities operate. It must be able to secure for itself the means for self-subsistence and self-maintenance, in order to function effectively as an independent social force. Left groups have to be able to determine the internal processes by which they reach their ideological position—subject only to the caveat that these processes respect the autonomy of the group's individual members. And, as with individual leftists, other groups must 'take them at their word' regarding how they decide the precise constellation of social concerns, values, identities, and societal dimensions they stand for.

In other words, cooperation between left groups and their organised agents must be rooted in the premise of mutual non-interference—or it is not truly *left* cooperation at all. Non-interference is also the only way of adequately incorporating the left's other social concerns. Interfering with the activism of other leftists or left groups denies them both the opportunity and the status of participating as equivalent forces in the left's fights for the disadvantaged and under-privileged. It immediately sets up a 'superior/inferior' relationship between different leftists, whereby some arbitrarily claim the mantle of ideological leadership and demand the others' acquiescence. Such interference is also a direct affront to tolerance, and sets itself against the diversity of left ideology in a way that explicitly—and somewhat hopelessly—denies the effects of complex differentiation in modern society. On all three counts, interference denies to fellow members of the left movement precisely what the movement as a whole is committed to securing for 'those without' in society.

In other words, people on the left must cooperate on the basis of mutual acknowledgment 'of each other as they find each other'. Of course, this does not in any way rule out intense and explicit expressions of mutual divergence, disagreement, and criticism between them. What is at stake in left disputes are crucial and his-torically-significant decisions over concerns, values, dimensions of identity, and domains of action—the cornerstones of left ideology. Disagreements over how these elements of left ideology should be understood, and the policies and strategies that ought to be pursued based on them, feed into decisions over the left's identity and status as a more-or-less coherent social movement. If these decisions are not co-formulated, pored over, commented on, and amended by as great a range of the left's members as possible, there will always be residual doubt about how far they truly live up to the left's social task.

But what is not at stake in left disputes are contingent personal or personnel questions regarding the members of left groups or their representative agents in organisations. Of course, individual people are the bearers of ideas and the performers of social practices—but people, ideas, and practices are not simply one and the same. A person's character is an insufficient guide to their abilities as an ideological activist. Nobody on the left should be basing their decision about whether, and how, to cooperate on mere questions of personalities. The point of the left is to fight for 'those without', and the sole criterion by which the left should be assessing opportunities for cooperation is by their ability to help them conduct this fight—i.e., to address social concerns and realise values wherever possible, across different dimensions of personal identity and across societal domains.

Left personnel appear only temporarily and in specific contexts, whereas left ideas are much longer-lasting. Individual personalities are too small-scale and contingent to be decisive for left groups' inherent or contextual ideological positions. Certainly, members of the left movement and their organised agents are hugely important *en bloc* to advancing left principles and goals by their activities. But from a macro-level perspective, in the grand sweep of society's history, they are largely interchangeable with one another. No single individual leftist, and no left group, has made so uniquely heroic a contribution that they did so totally devoid of others' help—or in a way that others could not have emulated, or done in their stead. To put it simply, ideologies and movements rely on *people*; they do not rely on *individuals*.

Further, structurally, personnel fall into the exclusive remit of autonomous left bodies. For groups within the left, which persons are and are not members is at best marginally a question of the group's choice. Far rather, it is individual persons who decide which groups they consider themselves to belong to, based on their personal identity, their role within societal domains, and so on. For the left's representative agents and organisations, meanwhile, the question of staffing—including selection, recall, etc.—forms part of the accountability processes towards 'their' groups. Only a mandating left group holds the ultimate ability to challenge or change the personnel who act as agents on its behalf. Beyond this link, in inter-agential and inter-organisational space, if agents or organisations want to cooperate, they cannot pick and choose which individual people they do or do not want to work with. Acknowledging other organisations 'as they find them' means taking these organisations 'as a whole'.

Overall, the key for the left to understand itself as a movement is to shift away from the cultish fixation on individualism and person-alities. Progressive concerns and values cannot be reduced to merely the personal will, intentions, or ideas of a single figure or a narrow group. The clearest reason for this is the sheer partiality of any single individual's perspective. Even a highly-committed left activist with intense personal experience of being 'without' on various dimen-sions, or in several domains, still cannot personify the entirety of the left movement. It is not possible to extrapolate anything from any one leftist's power, structural position, attitude, or behaviour about those of any other leftist or of the left movement as a whole. The same is true of any one leftist's particular 'spin' on the values of equality, justice, solidarity, and so on. The only proper approach is to look at the left on aggregate, and take into account as far as possible all leftists' different contributions.

The left needs to recognise the dangers to the realisation of its own values of synonymising the left movement (or particular left groups and organisations) with the personal following of any single left-wing individual. Any totalising identification with even rightly influential figures within the movement grants them excessively-concentrated control in shaping the ideological character of the organisations they belong to. This is a vastly retrograde step from the perspective of emancipation, as it denies ordinary members' ability to contribute to the ideological trajectory of the group and its representative organisations. Likewise, it limits the capacity for these organisations to maintain an adequate degree of internal pluralism, since it makes members' individual constellation of concerns, values, identities, and domains of action subservient to that of elite figures. Instead, the membership of a left group, and the mass support it offers its agents, should be just as important as its organisations' leadership elite—if not strictly more.[1] As the people whom the organisations are notionally representing, all members of left groups should be of equal standing as far as taking into consideration their needs and interests is concerned. And it is only through the inclusive mechanisms of mass participation that left groups can adequately support their members' attempts to bring these needs and interests to the attention of the movement as a whole.

The left must avoid situations where debates over the merits or demerits of particular individuals become a cipher for broader struggles between different ideological tendencies within and between left groups and organisations. Disagreements over priorities, interpretations, and emphases do not begin and end with personnel. Individuals only reflect—or are mandated to represent—various ideological positions, which circulate among the left movement at large. It is up to (other) autonomous left group members to decide whether they want to exclude, or recall, those individuals if they no longer consider them to be adequately representative of them, or aligned with their cause. The situation can be compared to the imperative need (discussed earlier) to avoid blurring together disputes over issues and disputes between entire outlooks. Neither specific situations nor specific people reflect movements in their entirety, and the left must avoid falling into the trap of reducing ideological trends to specific cases.

The danger is that, just like historical disputes, individual incompatibilities stand in the way of future cooperation between left groups and their organised agents. Again, the left cannot act as if personnel disputes do not exist. At the same time, it must accept that personal disputes *is all they are*. It cannot simply hope that they disappear, as they might instead be 'handed down' to subsequent generations of leftists, leading to factional strife. And it cannot keep obsessively returning to them, as this embeds them as a dividing line between ideological tendencies well after the people involved are long forgotten. In the same way, the left must also seek to resolve and overcome, rather than suppress or reanimate, disputes over personalities in the interest of carrying on and moving forward as a movement.

The left's overriding approach should be that no person is bigger than the ideology, and none is bigger than the movement. On that basis, it becomes very important for the left to know precisely how far any individual or group can be useful to furthering left aims, whether as ordinary members or organised agents. This requires each group to reflect on the parameters of its own 'leftness'—policing its boundaries, and constantly reevaluating its commitments to signal left concerns and values. For groups themselves, this becomes a question of whether their members continue to associate with one another, or whether they choose to dissociate and form separate groups. For these groups' agents, these concerns should be factored into the processes and considerations for determining their representative capacity and accountability—i.e., whether they are still 'up to' the job they are mandated to perform.

Part of being progressive is knowing when the movement has outgrown particular individual figures within it, as well as how to go about transcending and moving on from them. In general, this is a matter of finding the correct balance between the left's inherent (transcontextual) ideological identity—reflected in the movement—and its circumstantial (contextual) manifestation—embodied in the individual people in question. That is to say, the left needs to work out which side of this balance a given person represents better: left 'tradition' or left 'momentary need'. But this also becomes a matter of correct timing. The left needs to gauge carefully when a context has passed and become a different context, and hence when, or whether, the moment trumps tradition (and vice versa). The outcome of this assessment will determine when, and whether, the left decides to go for continuity or discontinuity in its personnel.

Relatedly, the left needs to find a consistent and frictionless approach to settling the transitions and handover processes between its time-limited 'torchbearers'. It is of paramount importance to avoid the chaotic infighting and recriminations that often accompany contested or incompletely-accepted decisions about whether to retain or change personnel. The left's efforts here must be targeted at preventing these challenges from metastasising into full-scale crises for the left movement or its representative organisations. The sequential succession of left personnel needs to maintain fluidity but avoid impermanence, and at the same time maintain stability but avoid ossification. This means that the left needs to systematise the basic rationales for both continuity and discontinuity. It must stipulate clearly the conditions for success (and hence continuation) and failure (and thus discontinuation) for both its ordinary members and organised agents—beyond mere informal or habitual enforcement (e.g., after general election defeats).

Both continuity and discontinuity can be subtle, resembling more a 'reshuffle' than a 'purge'. Above all, the left needs to avoid any toxic and unstable oscillation between the extremes of derivative mimicry and ostentatious 'clean breaks'. It also has to explicitly decouple personnel changes from ideological shifts. Removing or replacing members and agents does not necessarily also mean wholly reevaluating the left's ideological outlook (on priority concerns, value conceptualisations, or identity/domain emphases) simply because those members and agents happened to share them. By the same token, keeping members and agents also does not necessarily mean that no ideological reevaluation is required whatsoever on their part, and for the movement as a whole. Either personnel changes or personnel retention may be necessary at different points to reduce or reinforce the appeal and prevalence of a given ideological outlook.

To bring about coherence in its policies and strategies at a level beyond interpersonal relations, the left needs proposals for how to disconnect personalities from ideological tendencies altogether. Especially where its members' choice of representative agents is concerned, the left has to make support for general ideological tendencies less contingent on support for particular candidates (and *vice versa*). In other words, the left requires mechanisms that can help avoid situations where an ideology 'stands or falls' with specific individuals. One part of the solution would be to institutionalise regular opportunities for left groups and organisations to reaffirm their personnel choices. These could take a similar form for all left organisational positions: interim votes of confidence or satisfaction in the individual's performance, periodic (i.e., regular but not excessively frequent) compulsory renomination and reselection processes, and significantly easier complaints and recall procedures.

The way to decrease the stakes for left groups and ideological tendencies in these votes and processes is to insulate the relative position of the faction to which the personnel belong from the outcome of these mechanisms themselves. Confidence, recall, and reselection processes could be kept separate, not least by introducing separate votes and different proportional thresholds to instigate each category of proceedings against the agent in question. Left groups could also ensure a degree of continued ideological incumbency for each position by having a slate of designated replacements or substitute candidates pre-nominated at the point of selection—such that the group only moves to reselection if an agent's replacement also fails confidence and recall votes. The overall aim of technical moves like these are to free debates within the left from the distraction of personal confrontations, and clear its path towards unhindered ideological development.

## NOTE

1. Antonio Gramsci, *Selections from the Prison Notebooks* (London: Lawrence & Wishart, 2005 [1929-35]); Karl Mannheim, *Ideology and Utopia* (London: Routledge, 1936 [1929]).

# PROTEST AND CONSTRUCTION

If the left wants to foster changes in society, what does it do to bring them about? Often, it can look as though the left's familiar, natural role is one of opposition and resistance. Certainly, framing society as a 'fight', a dichotomy between 'those with' and 'those without', sets up an asymmetric division within the population. Siding with 'those without' entails standing up to 'difficulties' in contemporary society. What the left fights *against* (oppression, hierarchy, discrimination, competition) takes analytical primacy in how the left sees the world—or, rather, those are the parts of the world that the left sees first. This is because, insofar as the world evinces what the left fights *for* (empowerment, parity, recognition, cooperation), it is not of urgent left concern, since it is already doing what the left thinks it ought to be doing anyway.

Embracing any values consistently entails finding things that are deficient because they contravene these values. Like the right and the centre, the left is often initially motivated by visceral (often emotional) responses to perceived 'bads' or 'evils' in society—anger, fear, hatred, disgust—with reasoning about their causes and the specific source of their negative character only coming at a later point.[1] These responses are the prerequisite for the left to develop concepts and values that both encapsulate what a 'good' alternative would look like and can inspire an opposite visceral attachment—enthusiasm, hope, love, attraction. At that point, current society becomes defined in terms of what it lacks, and becomes fair game for criticism on the basis that it lacks it. Equally, social progress receives both the motivation and the goal of improving how a society's members viscerally feel about it.

Diagnosis and critique are the inevitable starting-point for identifying lacks in the ideological or policy *status quo*. When we look at the world, we start out from negation. The kernel of the vision of society that the left wants to see is the removal of the kind of society it does *not* want to see. Of course, positive left action to form the 'good society' can ultimately go well beyond merely overturning the worst forms the 'bad society' currently takes. But before positive left action can get started on improving the world, it must first occupy itself with 'de-worsening' it. Among other things, before the pendulum can swing towards the left, it first has to swing away from the right and past the centre. And in order to achieve this effectively, the left needs to grasp what society is like as comprehensively and correctly as possible.

The point of resistance is that the left sees its concerns, and the absence of its values, as the results of 'positive' actions by others. The left is not just 'picking a fight' with some natural state of affairs, or artificially upsetting the balance in an otherwise calm, ordered society. Rather, it is reacting to changes in society that are being wrought by others who are not of the left. Left action is a 'fight' precisely because it is not operating in a passive environment, but constantly working against opposing actions from the centre and the right. These include, but are by no means limited to, attempts to safeguard the intergenerational inheritance of wealth and status privileges; to inject unregulated enterprise and market competition into every area of social life, no matter how inappropriate; to convert state institutions into little more than glorified security apparatuses to enforce 'law and order' at home and sovereign interests abroad; and, most perniciously, to create false equivalencies between those who seek to change the *status quo* to bring about a better future and those who aim to do so by 'turning back the clock' to a mythicised past. The left must constantly pre-empt, check, block the changes its opponents are trying to make to society—or, indeed, their efforts to prevent changes from happening. Its task is to positively undo the countervailing positive action of the 'non-left', insofar as it exacerbates what the left disapproves of in society.

But this is only a partial exercise of the left's social agency. The left must remember that, like all ideologies and movements, its ultimate task it not only to respond to but also to steer changes in society. If the left stays only at the level of diagnosis and critique, it continues to leave others (the centre, the right) in a position of primacy, or control, over the context that determines their activities. This limits the left to being permanently reactive. It forces it to act as if it is a passive observer, watching with palpable relief as progress mysteriously comes about of its own accord—rather than owning up to its role as the key originator and driver of such progress. More pointedly, it is an abrogation of both its ability and its responsibility to take charge of determining the course of history. The left cannot simply sit back and 'expect' progress. It has to actively 'make' progress instead.

In fact, the point of the left constituting itself as a movement and a set of ideologies at all is its commitment to a social vision that it *actively* works towards. Its concerns are to be addressed *through action*; likewise, it is only *through action* that its values are going to be realised. The whole point of conceiving society in terms of the need to 'fight' (for 'those without' and against their opponents among 'those with') is that the left is called to action regardless of whether it wants to or not. The fight is already here, the left just needs to decide how (not whether) to participate in it. Merely sticking to diagnosis and critique wastes the opportunity to 'win' fights rather than simply commenting on them, and risks 'losing' them by failing to intervene.

So what does it mean for the left to address its social concerns? First and foremost, the left needs to reject the apparent contradiction between fighting against power, hierarchical structures, discriminatory attitudes, and competitive behaviour and taking hold of or assuming them to use and wield them for its own ends. Ridding itself of thinking in terms of 'all-or-nothing' binaries is part of what the left must do to move away from any monistic purism about how (and which) social visions should be realised. At the very least in the short and medium term, the left must recognise that these concerns are ineradicable. They must be taken as largely given, in which context the left's task of societal transformation becomes about finding different purposes and approaches for them *within* the current societal set-up. Obviously, the left is broadly averse to maintaining and entrenching them as they are. But it is entirely capable of capturing and reimagining or subverting them to its own ends—and it should always remain open to doing so.

But even in the longer term, the left is not necessarily trying to abolish these social concerns, but to reduce, redistribute, reorient, or reorder them. Power will always continue to exist in society in a more or less concentrated form. The point of the left's activities is to transform who holds and wields it, for how long, for what purposes, and how they gained it. Similarly, structures are a vital part of 'settling' how people and groups relate to one another into even just a briefly lasting form. The left's aim is to loosen the grip that some groups currently have on the 'better' positions within them, and limit the costs for those who end up in 'worse' ones. And both discrimination and competition will keep lurking in the background as long as there are differences between people in society. The left's task is to diminish and marginalise both of them as the default way of coping with social differences for those who want to find an alternative, but it cannot rule out using them to protect itself from those who refuse to give up such divisiveness. As ever, the left needs to be amenable to operating at both levels, through the division of labour between left organisations—resisting their negative effects, but using their positive effects wherever possible.

Along the same lines, what does it mean for the left to realise its values? Left visions are ideals, not utopias.[2] They are not just alternative 'mirror' views of what society could look like. They are serious claims about what it *should* look like, setting ambitious targets for what it *will* look like in future. In other words, it is not enough for the left simply to define current society in terms of what it lacks and put forward a better alternative. By itself, that gives no sense of the relationship between the two—i.e., how remote and speculative, or how immediate and plausible the alternative is compared to where society is now. The left's task is one of active pursuit, not passive endorsement. Its values have to be able to motivate and inform an account of transformative stages (however incremental), and a sequence of goals (however ambitious)—each of which can be defined as realising left values in a particular way.

As well as this, left values are guiding principles for creative action. They are designed to inform not only its goals and the interim stages leading up to it, but also the tactics and strategy for getting there—how these goals and stages are joined up. This is the real core of arguing for the left not just to pursue negative protest but also positive construction. The left's values need to run continuously through every aspect of the left project, in order to ensure that the processes and strategies by which it achieves its goals actually *are* positive in the 'correct' (left) way, and do not fall into the category of the 'incorrect' (centre, right) positive actions that the left opposes and resists. This continuity is needed to make sure that what the left is doing actually is *constructive*, in the sense that the process of moving from stage to stage itself builds on the left's achievements up to that point.

On both fronts, the left needs to remember that its visions may well be comprehensive, but are not monolithic. Different dimensions of personal identity and societal domains present various degrees of necessities and opportunities to capture and subvert existing privilege. The ambition to find 'diverse' candidates (especially women, people of colour, or disabled) to fill existing job vacancies and staff positions is now increasingly well-established, while left history has showed the effectiveness of using parliamentary structures to gradually prise open absolutist governmental systems. Meanwhile, there is a limit to how far better working-class accessibility to well-paying jobs in business or banking can genuinely eradicate classist stratifi-cations, while it would take an extremely long march through reli-gious institutions to fully eradicate their residual heteropatriarchal tendencies. Likewise, dimensions of identity and societal domains offer varying prospects of engaging in constructive projects of cer-tain forms and on differing scales. It is, for instance, a fairly simple conceptual step to ensure gender parity within current employment structures, or to legislate for equal rights to marriage and family life for LGBTQ* people. It is a vastly more complex aim to overcome tensions between ethnic and religious communities, or to eliminate private and public schools from the education system. It may not always be possible to align them perfectly immediately, even if that is the left's eventual goal. This means that the left is confronted with forced choices of what to prioritise—which, in the end, is the source of most internal left disputes.

This is where a careful and considered relationship to the past and to society's historical trajectory comes back in. The left must be sensitive to differences across dimensions of identity and societal domains, and the historical reasons for why they exist. This requires the left to maintain an attentive balance between responding to and steering societal changes. When formulating every successive stage of progressive construction, the left must confront the question of urgency. Progress does not (and should not necessarily) take place at the same rate in every part of the social world, and the more complex society becomes, the more divergent these rates of prog-ress can become. What the left must so is ensure that no concern or value in any dimension or domain becomes excessively favoured or neglected—from the left's perspective, they are all pressing *by definition*, and none of them can be allowed to overshadow the oth-ers for too long.

Above all, the left is about making a tangible difference for 'those without' in society. This is why it is so important for the left to acknowledge precisely how its concerns and values differ and interrelate across the boundaries between different personal identities and societal domains. If it does not do this accurately and effectively, it is less able to fight for 'those without' in a way that actually improves their position in society. This is also the reason why the left needs to work towards achieving representation for every dimension of identity and in every domain, and organise its agents accordingly. In this respect, it is substantially better for the left to 'go overboard'. Its members should feel comfortable trying to be as far ahead of the curve as they can possibly be—seeking out ways of finding new identity- or domain-related 'angles' on its concerns and values. Again, this is not the left 'picking a fight'. By doing this, it is merely pre-empting and positioning itself for fights that are heading for it anyway.

Positive construction for the left partly relies on a complex form of entryism. The left must insert itself and its agents and organisations into every part of society, in order to be able to bring a left outlook to bear on 'how things are' within it—specifically, 'its' version of the general social relationship between 'those with' and 'those without'. The point to stress is that there is nothing whatsoever insidious about this approach. Entryism does not have to be clandestine infiltration, but can involve the open and legitimate occupation of conventional social roles. External shock events may cause large groups of people to suddenly flock to become members of particular parties or trade unions, customers and employees of certain companies, audiences of and contributors to individual media outlets, adherents of specific faiths, and so on. Every such change can transform the internal composition of the organisations in question—and such transformation may also quite legitimately carry in its wake a change in their ideological character. Society is saturated with contests between ideologies. It is never—and never has been—in a 'non-ideological' pristine state.[3] All the left is doing is ensuring it has a 'seat at the table' when these contests take place. On this basis, the left has to target all the possible accessible roles across society, including and especially those responsible for perpetuating differences between 'those with' and 'those without'. The left is not too good or righteous for any of them. *It cannot afford not to get its hands dirty.*

This returns us to the question of what the responsibilities of those who occupy and fulfil these roles are to 'their' parts of the left, and to the left as a whole. Ultimately, given that they have extensive self-determination, they owe self-awareness and self-reflection: regularly and rigorously checking and shoring up their own 'leftness'. In the first instance, this is a matter of careful *self-diagnosis* and *self-critique*. People on the left need to remain sensitive to how they use their power and structural position, what attitudes they have, and what behaviour they exhibit. They are justifiably expected not to engage in corrupt, cynical power-grabs for their own personal or factional gain; not to treat those around them with high-handedness or dismissive snobbery; not to judge them arrogantly; and not to damage or undermine them as a way to bring themselves success. In other words, they have to try and ensure that they do not themselves fall into what they by their own criteria would consider 'incorrect' approaches to social concerns, flouting the left values they espouse. Instead, they must consistently work to erode such approaches *in themselves* as well as in society at large.

But again, self-diagnosis and self-critique are not enough here either. Members of the left also need to engage in a process of positive *self-creation*. They must consciously seek out ways to shape how they use their power, structural position, attitudes, and behaviour so that in everything they do they foster and develop left approaches to social concerns, and enhance the realisation of left values in society. They can push for progressive changes to combat classism, sexism, racism, homophobia, etc., in their workplace, their place of study, their local area, and their family life. They can intervene to block or call out measures designed to perpetuate the privilege and advantage of 'those with', and dissolve institutions that foster it. And they can refuse to go along with measures that seek to pit them against their colleagues, neighbours, comrades, and friends. In other words, what every leftist owes—to society as a whole, and particularly to the disadvantaged and underprivileged and their allies within it—is (in stagewise sequence) to pursue left goals to their utmost ability within their own context, and to prefigure these goals as far as possible given the parameters of their role. Certainly, this is an ambitious expectation. But it is an essential part of the fight to which the left has committed itself.

This has one main purpose: if the left is going to take advantage of the opportunities that society in its current form offers to assume and wield power, hierarchical positions, discriminatory attitudes, and competitive behaviour, these must not be allowed to go to waste. To press home the point: there is nothing as such contradictory or hypocritical in a leftist taking a position in (e.g.) a hedge fund, a management consultancy, corporate law firm, armed forces section, tabloid newspaper, or any other body to whose social functions the left is traditionally opposed, *as long as that leftist is reasonably confident that they will still be able to use that position to seriously and meaningfully pursue left goals.* More generally, it is vital to avoid a dangerous, toxic divide emerging between 'institutional' and 'extra-institutional' sections of the left, since this can only lead to the frustration of the left's aims as a movement, and guarantee the victory of the centre and the right. These responsibilities of self-diagnosis, self-critique, and self-creation are meant to help ensure that the activities of the 'institutional' left continue to broadly reflect the original reasons for protest and resistance by their 'extra-institutional' comrades. Obviously, processes of recall and reselection are the ultimate formal check on this. But that is a 'sledgehammer' approach, whereas the 'scalpel' version is simply to demand that leftists stringently adhere to certain norms of conduct.

The left also needs to recognise that these responsibilities fall collectively on the left movement as much as personally on individual leftists. It is entirely possible, even likely, that no single left member or agent may be capable of meeting their responsibilities consistently on their own—even if they are entirely well-intentioned, and stringently mandated to do so. Ideological contestation seeps into every pore of social life; the fight against right-wing, reactionary inclinations is one that everyone faces within their own psyches too.[4]

This is a major part of why left strategy requires organic coordination and coalition-building between left agents in (even potentially contradictory) social roles, to maximise the links between people engaged in left constructive projects. Even if individuals 'fall short' for whatever reason, others can take up the slack on behalf of the movement as a whole, so that the overarching left project is not halted or set back.

Although there may well be a division of activities between leftists who are more concerned with diagnosis and critique, and other leftists who are more concerned with construction, the left needs to try and maintain a healthy degree of contact and reciprocity between them. Left thinkers who never lift a finger to try and improve society are no better than left activists who never pause to take stock of the state it is in. It is crucial that the left strengthen the bridge between the practical activities associated with each side of this division. This is true both in terms of how leftists should think about moving from the negative to the positive aspects of their activities on a personal level, and within and between different left groups and agents who have specialised on either side.

It is important for the left to recognise that none of its members may ultimately be capable of striking a perfect individual balance between protest and resistance on the one hand, and creative action on the other. What matters is that the left as an ideological movement attains something close to the right balance between them *as a whole*. To do so, it may need to rely on mutual processes of 'checking' and monitoring between the left groups and their organised agents that have sprung up for every dimension of personal identity, and in every social domain. Such frameworks for internal and external auditing and scrutiny create formal, transparent mechanisms for members of the left to 'call out' and offer feedback on how others use their social roles to further left goals. They can help the left denounce and rectify failures to use these roles adequately or appropriately, but also to exchange 'best practices' and refine the efficacy of left action in society.

## NOTES

1. Antonio Damasio, *Descartes' Error* (New York, NY: Quill, 2000); Daniel Goleman, *Emotional Intelligence: Why it can matter more than IQ* (London: Bloomsbury, 1996).

2. David Estlund, 'Utopophobia', *Philosophy and Public Affairs* 42(2) (2014), 113-34; Charles Mills, 'Ideal Theory as Ideology', *Hypatia* 20(3) (2005), 165-83; Ingrid Robeyns, 'Ideal Theory in Theory and Practice', *Social Theory and Practice* 34(3) (2008), 341-62.

3. Ernesto Laclau, 'The Death and Resurrection of the Theory of Ideology', *Journal of Political Ideologies* 1(3) (1996), 201-20; Aletta Norval, 'The Things We Do with Words: Contemporary Approaches to the Analysis of Ideology', *British Journal of Political Science* 30(3) (2000), 313-46; Slavoj Žižek (ed.), *Mapping Ideology* (London: Verso, 1994).

4. Mark Fisher, *Capitalist Realism* (Ropley: Zero Books, 2009).

# DISCUSSION AND DECISION

**W**hen should the left switch from discussion to decision? This question taps into a lingering point of potential tension between the left's value-commitment to pluralism and the strategic aspiration of unity. First and foremost, the left's determination to fight for 'those without' and against 'those with' (unless they side with 'those without') means it has a 'bottom-up' approach to discovering and developing its social concerns and values. These are rooted in the interests of the mass, given that in all forms of society up to now 'those without' have always vastly outnumbered 'those with'. The left is more interested in 'ordinary' people's thinking than the *ex cathedra* wisdoms of individual 'great thinkers'—which are primarily a fetish of the liberal centre and conservative right. Of course, it makes some exceptions in cases where certain individuals happen to have grasped some part of mass thinking particularly effectively—such as, for example and in no particular order, Karl Marx, the Pankhursts, Eduard Bernstein in debate with Rosa Luxemburg, Walter Lippmann in debate with John Dewey, Frantz Fanon, Mahatma Gandhi, Betty Friedan, Judith Butler, and Kimberlé Crenshaw. But this is by no means the mainstay of the left's pool of ideas, and every time it defers to such canonical figures, it slightly sacrifices its 'bottom-up' credentials.

The left starts its focus at the bottom of society—those who are 'with' the least (privilege, advantage), or those who are the most 'without'—and gradually works its way up from there. This superficially straightforward approach is made vastly more arduous by the growth and complexification of society. The proliferation of dimensions of personal identity and societal domains with respect to which people can be 'with' or 'without' essentially breaks down any chance of automatic homogeneity of 'mass' interests and thinking. The left's task moves from simply aggregating and amplifying the mass's views to carefully negotiating the fault-lines within and between them. Obviously, the left's goal is to accommodate areas of intersection—mitigating where they cross-cut, nurturing them where they align. But the prerequisite for doing so is investing significant time and effort in paying attention to each one of these proliferating and diverging experiences and perspectives. Quite simply, the left cannot claim to be an inclusive movement if it does not do so.

The discussion of ideas is one of the key areas where the left can, and must, prefigure society as it wants it to be.[1] That is to say: left discussion cannot just be substantively about left social concerns and values as they manifest for different identities and in different societal domains—it must also procedurally reflect them at every point. It must allow participants to access the informational and rhetorical resources they need to make insightful, eloquent contributions to the discussion. Left discussion spaces and contexts must be arranged in a way that minimises deferential formalities and prevents individual participants from derailing or commandeering the discussion's trajectory. Left discussion must respect the dignity and ability of all participants to authentically articulate their views and represent their own ideological positions. And it has to stringently avoid debate and collective reflection descending into divisive arguments that are geared towards certain participants achieving a sectional ideological hegemony. Discussion is typically the initial 'front' where proposals to radically transform society are first broached, so transforming the way it takes place is a valuable initial step towards encouraging further progressive proposals to be put forward.

This relies on the left creating discussion spaces that strictly conform to its values as they affect debate and deliberation—even if
this comes across as stilted from the perspective of how discussions
take place 'normally'. In left discussions, the status of participants
must be homogeneously standardised and universalised across all
those who claim it, and they must be assured as far as possible that
they get out of discussions exactly what they need from taking part
in them. These discussions must allow people to exercise free speech
in the sense of 'free*ing* speech', in that the processes and contexts of
discussion themselves must be emancipatory. They must accommodate the range and variety of views and perspectives that participants
hold, while recognising that they all have to be aiming for resolu-
tions that meet all of their interests as far as possible—specifically
by achieving improvements in their lives and those of the people
they are 'speaking for'.[2]

It is worth going into more detail on various aspects of left discussion. To start with: who participates in it? The answer is superficially
simple: left discussion should be designed to include 'those without'
and their allies among 'those with'. But in order to ensure that 'those
without' are guaranteed participation in these discussions, the left's
form of inclusion must go beyond the 'universal formal access'
granted to them alongside 'those with' as co-members of any population group by centre or right interpretations. Left inclusion has to
take the form of prioritising 'those without'. Left discussion should
start with the perspectives of 'those without', and centrally feature
individual members of 'those without', on the basis that they are
best-placed to articulate these perspectives authentically and rep-
resentatively on behalf of themselves and others in a like position.
Only then may it expand the circle of inclusion to add the perspectives of 'those with' on the same issues.

Where does left discussion take place? Again, the initial answer
is deceptively simple: left discussion can potentially be found anywhere in society. Since the left can penetrate into any part of society, it is feasible for disadvantaged people with different identities
and in different domains to start developing left ideas and practices

in response to issues that arise within their personal contexts. But therein lies the key factor that the left must take to heart: it is precisely in contexts where left concerns arise and left values are found wanting that left discussions are most likely to emerge. It is members of social groups who are 'close to' these contexts—who are at the direct receiving end of the disadvantaging and depriviledging effects of power, structures, attitudes, and behaviour in their parts of society—who will be the first to consider how to fight against them. In other words, the left must recognise that experience breeds understanding—and that the most promising sources of innovative left ideas are the people at the forefront of left activism.

What does the left discuss? In some respects, the answer is obvious: the left discusses its concerns and values as they pertain to different personal identities and societal domains, how its ideas relate to its practices, and how to convert its principles into strategies. Yet buried in this self-evident observation is the kernel of a vital point: for a discussion to be 'left' it must be about the left's fundamental preoccupation, the fight for 'those without', and against the harmful activities of 'those with'. Anyone who participates in a discussion that does not directly tackle this preoccupation is not, to that extent, in a *left* discussion. This is true even if they are a member or agent of the left, if they are discussing unrelated topics—sport, music, arts and culture, day-to-day events, etc., though even here there is still a lurking chance that the struggle between 'those with' and 'those without' will suddenly rear its head. More pressingly, anyone who brings (e.g., centre, right) views that ignore or reject the terms of the left's fundamental fight to a notionally left discussion should be regarded by the left as challenging and undermining its 'leftness'. The discussion can evidently go ahead, but the left must remain sensitive to how the introduction of such views changes its ideological integrity—and, importantly, how it 'crowds out' the issues faced by 'those without' from the discussion space.

How does left discussion take place? The left's views on the who, where, and what of left discussion have a profound impact on how it prefigures the conduct of discussions in future society as the left conceives of it. Certainly, it should reflect the left's social concerns and values—but, like left cooperation, left discussion cannot be self-defeating. The generous terms of (e.g.) equality, freedom, and pluralism on which left discussion is to take place should only be applied to views, and people, who are prepared to extend the same terms to others in the discussion. This should be the case automatically for all consistent and conscientious leftists, but may also include centrists and rightists who are prepared to abide by these terms. In this respect, left discussion should be seen as a model for how every other form of left activity might take place: the left's terms of conduct apply only to those who accept them, and are extended to others outside the left insofar as they engage with the left 'in good faith'.

Why does the left discuss? At this point, it is helpful to offer a brief reminder of what left discussion—like the left's other activities—is ultimately meant to achieve. The left's ambition is to steer the deep changes in society in a progressive direction: to turn time's arrow from merely forward to upward by improving the situation of 'those without'. To do so, it aims to both build on and overcome the past and present. This gives the left a clear preference for discussions that have a forward orientation, which feature views that have yet to assert themselves in social debates, and which set out to achieve shared goals to foster the better development of society. In turn, this strongly suggests that the left should categorically reject discussions with an opposite aim—a backward orientation, hoping to revert to the understandings of the past, or any attempt to frustrate the achievement of developmental goals. The treatment of history is a vital criterion for how the left should assess people and their views, since it can be used in various ways to legitimise ideological perspectives that are not always conducive to progressive aims.

Together, these point towards a clear code of conduct that orients the left's approach to ideological discussion. The left's position comes down to the observation that social views are not marginalised if the people who hold them form a technical numerical minority in the population, but rather if the people who hold them are overwhelmingly disadvantaged or underprivileged within society. Freedom to speak in left discussions does not strictly have to involve curbing the speech of 'those with', but it should inversely track the asymmetries of privilege and advantage in society. The left's stance is that the views of 'those with' are simply less of a priority. Instead, the discussions to which it must pay particular attention are those that take place in social groups that predominantly comprise the disadvantaged and underprivileged, and within their representative organisations. The left must also move away from the idea that all views are equivalent, and instead emphasise those that seek to keep in check and diffuse the advantage and privilege of 'those with', while counteracting the disadvantage and underprivilege of 'those without'. The core point is that the left should abandon the assumption that giving views equivalent consideration translates into blanket tolerance for all views, or guaranteed civil treatment for all those who hold and express them. The identity of people and the substance of their views matters. In particular, left discussion must only give views consideration if they are demonstrably intended to turn societal changes to the ultimate advantage of 'those without'. The reasoning is simple: if the left's mission is to eradicate classism, sexism, racism, homophobia, transphobia, ableism, and xenophobia in society, then it serves no plausible purpose for its discussions to be opened up to views that defend their continued existence.

These principles for discussion are essential for the left to abide by if it is to stand the best possible chance of formulating principles and strategies that can achieve social progress. But the left also has to bear in mind the need to 'lock in' this progress. No matter how democratic and deliberative a left group or organisation is, it is unalterably the case that effective left action requires a point of *cloture*—a suspension of discussion over ideas in favour of making a decision about practices. In order to address their concerns clearly, and realise their values consistently, left groups and their organised agents need a settled ideological 'line'.[3] This can be as nuanced and carefully developed as they want it to be—but it needs to be framed as an (at least temporary) 'conclusion', closed to discussion and left unchallenged for some amount of time. Here, ideology and activism go 'hand in hand', mutually reinforcing and influencing one another. Simply put, ideological confusion breeds uncertain and incoherent activism, and ideological clarity makes activism effective and well-defined.

This unavoidable break between discussion and decision echoes the division between diagnosis and critique, and creative construction. Both are examples of a division of labour within the left's activities. Yet these divisions are not identical. It is self-evidently possible to have both discussions that are diagnostic or critical, and also ones that veer more towards the constructive side. Much of left journalism and academia falls into the former category, as it commentates on the *status quo*, or dissects its theoretical and empirical dimensions, while left policy research is often more concerned with the latter task. Similarly, decisive action can plainly also come in diagnostic/critical and constructive forms. Left protests, strikes, rallies, occupations, and other forms of civil disobedience and unrest are largely geared towards disrupting the *status quo*, while it is the more nuanced and painstaking process of drafting legislation, fundraising, pitching proposals and lobbying, counselling, education, and so on, that are the ways to building a new *status quo* entirely. It is part and parcel of the increasing specialisation in modern complex society that, alongside differentiation in personal identities and societal domains, different parts of the left lean towards different combinations of these two divisions as well. The shifts between diagnosis/critique and construction, and from discussion to decision, are two further examples of growing social intricacy that the left as a movement must bridge in order to keep itself united and coherent.

Altogether, the left will always find itself facing the four strategic choices outlined in the previous four chapters: between preserving and abandoning the past, maintaining or moving on from personnel, diagnosis/critique versus construction, and discussion versus decision. To varying degrees of intensity, the left also shares these choices with the centre and the right—and it is partly in the alignments and overlaps between them that the key to cooperation beyond the left's borders lies. As with the other three choices, the left needs to remain highly sensitive to when it is the kairotic 'right time' to switch from discussion to decision, from the perspective of meaningfully achieving its goals.[4] This is ultimately a matter of finding a working balance between the left's commitment to recognition and pluralism, and keeping these within certain limits in favour of meeting other concerns—e.g., empowerment, cooperation—and realising other values—e.g., freedom, solidarity.

But likewise, just as in its other choices, the left must acknowledge that it is in a never-ending series of continuous cycles: preserving-abandoning, maintaining-moving on, critique-creation, and discussion-decision. The past cannot be ignored, but it cannot be allowed to overwhelm the present and the future. Personnel are important but not indispensable. Critical diagnoses are necessary but must not crowd out constructive alternatives. And discussions are key to informing decisions, but should never prevent these from being reached. Contingency is the lifeblood of social life, and the left must learn how to cope with the fact that its choices are only ever temporary, never final.[5] The trick is trying to determine *what point it is at* as an ideological movement (in its many parts and levels) within each of these cycles, and what the right strategy for it to take is on that basis.

Developing left concepts and values should be an entirely pluralistic process. But enacting them forces leftists to make a reductionist—even singular—choice of some (one) over the others. The key for the left is to ensure that such choices do not excessively and irreversibly sacrifice the richness of the preceding discussion, while also not letting this richness overshadow the imperative to 'get things done'. Certainly, even the most resolutely closed discussions can be reopened later, and even the firmest decisions can subsequently be counteracted (if not strictly undone). Yet in the interim, at the moment of choice, the left needs procedures that institutionally prevent any left member or agent from carrying either too far at the expense of the other. This accommodation is a difficult balance to strike. But left organisations are frankly incomplete if they cannot guarantee three things: complete pluralism of views before the decisive moment; adherence to a 'party line' after it; and an option to change it by reopening sensitive or controversial issues for debate.

Many of these accommodations already take place in an *ad hoc*, informal fashion at the level of left groups and individual agents. These constantly oscillate back and forth between deliberative discussion and decisive action, often without the need for designated moments of 'switchover', and systematic rules for doing so. But this is much more challenging in the case of representative organisations. Not least due to the complexity and significance of their specialised tasks, these rely on usually highly-stylised processes for opening and closing discussions, and taking or revising decisions. Typically, these organisations rely on some kind of convention to make these choices, either of a full organisational congress or conference, or at least a meeting of a relevant policy or executive committee. But these processes are not always equally balanced between the three guarantees the left must offer, and sometimes deeply opaque and inaccessible to the organisations' mandating left groups. This, before anything else, is what the left must remedy in order to return control of its ideological direction as a movement firmly to the hands of its members.

## NOTES

1. Jon Elster (ed.), *Deliberative Democracy* (Cambridge: Cambridge University Press, 1998); Amy Gutmann and Dennis Thompson, *Democracy and Disagreement* (Cambridge, MA: Belknap Press, 1998); Michael A. Neblo, *Deliberative Democracy between Theory and Practice* (Cambridge: Cambridge University Press, 2015).

2. Robert Paul Wolff, Barrington Moore, and Herbert Marcuse, *A Critique of Pure Tolerance* (Boston, MA: Beacon Press, 1969).

3. Vladimir Lenin, *What Is to Be Done? Burning Questions of Our Movement* (New York, NY: International Publishers, 1929 [1902]).

4. Michael Carter, 'Stasis and Kairos: Principles of Social Construction in Classical Rhetoric', *Rhetoric Review* 7(1) (1988), 97-112; Joanne Paul, 'The use of Kairos in Renaissance Political Philosophy', *Renaissance*

*Quarterly* 67(1) (2014), 43-78; Eric Charles White, *Kaironomia: On the will to invent* (Ithaca, NY: Cornell University Press, 1987)

5. Judith Butler, Ernesto Laclau, and Slavoj Žižek, *Contingency, hegemony, universality: contemporary dialogues on the left* (London: Verso, 2000); Richard Rorty, *Contingency, Irony, and Solidarity* (Cambridge: Cambridge University Press, 1989).

# IV

# Towards left unity

# UNITY IN DIFFERENT FORMS

What form should left unity take? As should have become clear from the previous chapters, one fact about contemporary society that is becoming ever more established, and ever more immutable, is that there is not just one 'left'. The deep changes that have taken place in society, the rise of new dimensions of personal identity, the self-assertion of ever more distinct societal domains all mean that the future of the left as a movement is one of necessary coexistence. This is as much coexistence between different parts of an expanding and increasingly byzantine network of overlapping left groups and their representative agents and organisations, as between a growing range of variant interpretations of a broad but nonetheless still recognisable left ideology. What this means is that the left needs to categorically abandon all attempts at achieving a monolithic unification. That is an outcome that has never actually been achieved historically, and is receding ever farther out of reach in future.

Insofar as the left has realised this, it has aimed to cobble together unity *ad hoc*. It has sought to entrench and constantly reaffirm the ties between existing groups and their organised agents. It has worked hard to create ties to new groups and agents sporadically as and when they emerge. Essentially, the left's logic has been one of trying to preserve and protect the contours of the left movement as the contemporary left has inherited it. Its members have attempted to defend and perpetuate a legacy that can be traced back to the foundations of the movement and the ideology, and then co-opt its newest manifestations into what already exists. But this approach is an unrationalised 'add-on' logic masquerading as organic development. It relies on grafting or bolting new members of the left onto the existing systems and structures of the left movement, without holistically reconsidering what these new emergences mean for the overall picture of 'left-ness'.

This lends itself to a false unity, in the form of an ideological hegemony that is constantly on the back foot. It offers a totalising image of what the left 'is' (as opposed to what it 'does') that feels under relentless pressure to reassert and (at times) reinvent itself again and again. *Ad hoc* unity approaches subscribe to a logic of precedence, predominance, and primacy that falls foul of pretty much every left social concern to some degree. They rely on established left groups and organisations begrudgingly ceding control of activist resources to newcomers, and expecting these new arrivals to quietly 'slot into' a supporting role within the left's existing bodies, procedures, and institutions. They see the relative importance of the different dimensions of personal identity as inherently fixed—e.g., 'the primacy of class', or views that rank biological sex over gender identity—as opposed to contingently variable by context. And they are conditioned to view innovative understandings of concerns and values that emerge from newly salient identities or recent developments in societal domains as a *de facto* challenge to the left movement's established way of doing things.

It goes without saying that these reactive, reactionary approaches are a far cry from how left unity should be brought about. Left unity needs to be based on intelligent, case-specific alignment of activities, conciliation of interests, and a minimisation of areas of tension and conflict between its different 'moving parts'. Activist resources need to be mobile and accessible to all left groups and organisations, so that they can be fluidly deployed where (and by whom) they are needed most at any given time. The left's institutions and procedures cannot be allowed to ossify, but need to be constantly tested and revisited to ensure that they are not routinely neglecting any disadvantaged or underprivileged group in society. The left movement needs to become far more flexible in the 'lenses' through which it sees social issues, and stop assuming that every concern and value is automatically best assessed in terms of certain identities (e.g., class, gender, race) or best addressed in certain domains (e.g., politics, economics). And it must urgently drop its great misconception that left innovation necessarily comes at the cost of undermining, or eradicating, what went before.

The proliferation of left groups and their representative organisations is a source of both necessity and opportunity for the movement as a whole. Put simply, the deep changes in the character of society—changes the left is resolved to respond to and steer effectively—are forcing similar changes in the character of the left as well. The left is a more complex entity now than it was twenty, fifty, one hundred years ago. Its central activities and demographic contours have evolved, as have the organisations that provide the mainstay of its activism. And the only trajectory it has good reason to expect is one of yet more complexity, with a concomitant increase in the sheer number and diversity of its many 'moving parts'. As a result, left unity will have to overcome ever steeper and more insurmountable hurdles in future—and will become ever more urgently necessary for precisely that reason. There are no grounds for the left to assume that the forms of unification that have worked in the past will still be fit for purpose in its future fights. Rather, it must learn to embrace the need to experiment and innovate rather than retreating to familiar turf, to avoid risking a slow, grinding decline into social irrelevance.

At the same time, it is precisely from the left's increasingly numerous and diverse 'moving parts', operating quasi-autonomously and in a decentralised way, that the experimental innovations the movement needs are most likely to emerge. Every new area of left activism adds to the list of potential opportunities for cross-fertilisation as it intersects with existing areas. Anytime the left takes up position on the concerns of oppression, hierarchy, discrimination, and competition as they affect people disadvantaged because part of their personal identity has taken on some new social significance, its activities in fighting for them shed new light on the nature of the left, its ideas and practices. This is what is meant by exercises such as 'gendering' class or 'queering' race—carefully and painstakingly exploring the intersecting experiences of people whose personal identities bridge multiple dimensions of 'being without'. Something very similar is true for the reciprocal transfers and flows between the left's parallel presences in different societal domains as they develop. The left must track the areas where these domains overlap—'political economy', 'legal culture', 'religious education', 'family law', 'healthcare policy', etc.—as the sites where left agents and organisations are most likely to cross paths, and where their ideas and strategies are best placed to inform each other's tasks.

Instead, the left must come to understand itself as a fluid social ecosystem. Returning to the point that it is less who we are than what we do that makes us left-wing, it is better if the left thinks of itself as a dynamic network of intersecting practices and polycephalous active bodies, rather than as a static entity with a fixed character. In this context, left unity also cannot be something fixed. It cannot be some overarching pristine arrangement that fixes the relations between its constituent parts in perpetuity. If the left is an organic creation—created by the members of the population who share 'left' concerns and values—then it must see itself as an organism in motion. Left unity is rather a way of shaping and understanding how these component parts act with and alongside each other. It describes a homology of orientation, a harmony of processes, but not an undifferentiated block.

For the same reasons, the left must be understood—and must understand itself—as a confederal entity. As a movement, it has to be a loose configuration of grouped members and their organised agents, since crucially it operates on many very different social scales, in terms of both space (geography) and time. Left unity needs to respect the context-dependence and the autonomy of the left's constituent parts. Of course, it can be institutionalised in the form of congresses, committees, and other similar bodies that are designed to smooth the process of left-left cooperation. But these are 'bottom-up' creations by the different parts of the left acting in concert, not an ideological 'centre' to which these parts are subordinated. In turn, this means that left unity has to rely on quite a pared-down list of concerns and values, to ensure that there is still some common transcontextual and intertemporal pattern that lets all the parts still be meaningfully categorised as parts of the left.

Bearing all of this in mind, how should the left go about starting projects of left unity? Here, the key guiding principle must be: *start small*. It is far easier, and usually more effective, to begin such unification projects with experimental test cases, involving a limited number of people, over a limited time, and for limited purposes. They should concentrate on overcoming or conciliating rifts within the left caused by past crises, rather than immediately confronting new disputes. They should begin as agreed divisions of labour between specific individual left activists, rather than rushing to form left organisational coalitions straightaway. They should focus on mobilising together for protest and resistance before attempting to form grand new projects of construction. And they should prioritise participating in principled discussions together, and not promptly try to bind one another to a common programme of decisive strategies.

What all of these contrasts share is that they try to arrange the goals of the different parts of the left movement by ascending scale and scope of their cooperative ambitions. This is necessary because, in a society pervaded by oppression, hierarchy, discrimination, and especially competition, left groups and organisations face an extra hurdle in building up mutual trust and experience of acting together. Left unity should thus begin with issue-specific cooperation before embarking on comprehensive schemes of societal transformation. It should initially be treated as a contingent occurrence, and only later proposed in a more general, permanent form. Its scale should begin at the most microscopic level—e.g., local, among individual union and party branches, workplace and staff forums, faculty panels, etc.,

on individual questions and topics of coincidental shared interest—
and only then take on an increasingly macroscopic existence—e.g.,
regional, national, international, within entire companies, centres,
departments, and universities, or across entire industries, social sec-
tors, and ideological movements. And, of course, it should always
first be trialled informally before moving to institutionalise it in the
left's organisations.

There are a large range of possible unity projects, which can be
categorised according to three criteria. The first is their *intensity*:
how much, or how deeply, the various sides participating in them
unite into a single social entity. Between full mutual independence
and complete elision, there are several forms of cooperation that
fulfil the role of a 'left front' or 'popular front'. At the weakest and
most temporary end, groups can negotiate agreements with one
another for certain purposes: truces to suspend competition between
them, pacts to confirm that both will carry out particular activities, and other quasi-contractual bargains aimed at reducing mutual
interference of needs and interests. More intense are alliances and
coalitions, which introduce a significant degree of coordination and
conscious alignment into groups' activities, either during or after
hard-fought ideological (often political) 'campaigns'. At the highest and most lasting end, of course, are wholesale mergers of group
memberships and organisational structures. Not every form of unity
will serve the left's purpose in every context. But as a rule, the left
should always seek to forge truces and pacts wherever possible as
a way to 'get by' in ideological competition, and remain open to
expanding these into alliances, coalitions, and even mergers further
down the line.

The second criterion of unity is *extensity*: who the sides participating in unity projects actually are. This is significantly dependent on
what each project's purpose or delineated remit is: intuitively, the
more expansive or detailed a project's aims, the more likely it is that
would-be participants differ ideologically on the issues associated
with them. Groups and organisations are best placed to find ideological rivals willing to unite with them on individual points of concern

or general expressions of values—where overlap can happen despite otherwise ferocious ideological disagreement. The more they try to turn these points and expressions into extensive or precisely-defined ideological programmes, the more these groups will be forced to rely on others who share their more immediate ideological neighbourhood and kinship. Both point-by-point and programmatic unity are valid tactics for the left to pursue, depending on the context. In both cases, the left must acknowledge the trade-offs between extensity and ideological specificity that accompany each of these approaches, and decide what balance of the two every social situation requires.

Finally, unity projects can be assessed according to their *timescale*: how quickly they take place, in what order of internal steps, and over what period. The deciding factor here is the complexity and urgency of the contingent issue that makes social groups and organisations feel the need to consider unity at all. In some cases, groups notice themselves growing closer and more aligned in their perspectives over a longer period of ideological contestation over a range of successive issues. In other cases, groups may suddenly, even unexpectedly, find themselves on the same side of a stark division within society over a given issue. The process and timing of unification is utterly different between the two. Cases of the former type leave space for careful planning and preparation, and if unity comes about it is often the result of protracted and painstaking negotiation. The latter cases do not afford this luxury, and unity may be spontaneous and recklessly *ad hoc*, with only a superficial basis in discussion. The left must, of course, be open to either option. But it must always be mindful of one caveat: in order for the construction of any sort of unity to be stable, each step in the process needs to build clearly and logically on the previous ones, however quickly they follow each other.

On all three levels, the crucial question is how such unity projects acquire and sustain a left-wing character. The agreement (as far as it goes) between different leftists must be cemented with a settled shared programme, however formalised and formulated. Such a programme has to offer a simple set of 'ground rules' by which all parties to the agreement can abide. It must stipulate what is explicitly agreed on, and what activities all sides jointly commit to. It needs to pin down (inclusively and exclusively) how, as a united bloc, they view and intend to address social concerns, how they interpret and mean to apply values, and on which identities and in which domains their efforts are going to be focused. Certainly, the members of such unity projects have to be prepared to subscribe to *left* social concerns and values, broadly construed. But they do not have to have exactly the same views on them, with completely identical emphases. Their strategies and goals just need to be similar enough for cooperation between them to be possible and meaningful.

By the same token, any unity programme also has to stipulate for each of these cases what is left to be disputed or disagreed on, and where room is left for mutual difference between the various cooperating sides—as has happened most recently in the Portuguese *geringonça* ('contraption') coalition between social democrats, socialists, and green-communists.[1] Specifically, this includes which past disputes between them are left *unresolved*, which of their personnel is *not* expected to collaborate, and which projects are left at the level of diagnosis/critique and discussion rather than creative construction and decisive action. This should ideally be done explicitly rather than implicitly. For a unity project to work effectively, it is vital for all sides to have a clear basis for mutual trust, and a common gauge by which to assess the success or failure of their cooperation. Evidently, the aspiration with all such projects is that, over time, the length of this list of exclusions decreases as the cooperating sides build up trust towards one another.

All in all, the need for left unity is becoming increasingly unarguable. What the left as a movement needs to determine is how best to streamline the formation of these types of unity arrangements. There is no centralised body that can do this on behalf of the movement as a whole. Every part of the left, from individual leftists through groups all the way up to major organisations of left agents, must take up this task for themselves and in their own authentic way. Each must formulate and internally settle a system of preliminary expressions of intent to cooperate, which explicitly consider and outline with whom, in what way, and to what ends each of them is prepared to cooperate and unify. These sorts of reflections are an unavoidable part of such agreements being formed. It is only a matter of strategic forethought that lets the various parts of the left conduct these reflections ahead of time, without the pressure of urgent decision (to cooperate/unify or not), to facilitate the process of negotiation when it actually takes place.

Currently, the left negotiates with itself with the same degree of suspicion and resentment it reserves for the centre and the right. This manifestly goes against the realities of the ideological spectrum. By far the left's best hope for turning society in the direction it hopes for is rediscovering what holds it together as a movement. In the end, the left's decisive consideration—the one that unarguably trumps all others—is its commitment to fighting for 'those without' in society. They are the arbiters of its achievements, and their benefit is the summary criterion of its success. It is for their sake that the left must actively find ways to bolster its cohesion, in the face of social forces determined to worsen their situation from its already precarious state. Only through unity can the left meet head-on the threats that currently confront society—meet them adaptably, effectively, and at the pinnacle of its available strength.

## NOTE

1. Joana Ramiro, 'Why the left is continuing to win in Portugal', *New Statesman*, 9 October 2019; Peter Wise, 'Europe's socialist success story: the strange rebirth of the Portuguese left', *New Statesman*, 28 March 2018.

# CONCLUSION

## Ten Lessons for a Progressive Alliance

1. *The left* — Every social institution with more than 50 members creates a forum for each legally protected demographic characteristic (i.e., sex, gender, race and ethnicity, religion, sexual orientation, disability, marital and family status, and age). Membership of these forums is automatically open to all members of the institution (employees, etc.) who share the relevant characteristic, on an 'opt-in' basis. These forums are hosted by chairpersons elected by their members. These chairpersons automatically also become members of a mandatory Members' Council for each institution, where they represent their forums and provide consultation and oversight to the institution's operations. A predefined number of these Council members also join the institution's executive leadership (e.g., by sitting on the board of directors) as 'diversity reps', where they provide intersectional 'co-determination' in the running of the institution on behalf of its members.

2. *Left agents and institutions* — Every organisation that agrees with left social concerns and left values, which represents one or more groups with legally protected demographic characteristics elects delegates to a joint Progressive Congress, on a voluntary

basis. This Congress is to meet regularly, and brings together left agents who are active across all parts of society (e.g., in politics, the economy, law, religion, culture, education, etc.). The purpose of this Congress is to give left agents the opportunity to exchange and align their activities across social divides. It will also debate motions for changes to left policy and strategy, to help guide and coordinate activists in different parts of society. These are non-binding on participating organisations, but will be given added weight by having been endorsed by representatives of the left from across society at a national level.

3. *Parties and partisanship* — Every left-aligned political party amends its rulebook or constitution to permit its members to also be members of other parties. The list of allowed further memberships may be completely open, or as a second-best may be restricted to a specific list of alternative parties (e.g., as with the Labour and Cooperative parties). There are no restrictions on members participating fully in the activities of any or all the parties to which they belong. Candidates for political offices are allowed to campaign on a joint ticket, on consultation with the parties of which they are members (e.g., Labour-Women's Equality Party, SNP-Scottish Green, Liberal Democrat-Plaid Cymru). If elected, they take the whip of all the parties to which they belong; in effect, they act as 'Independents' or cross-benchers who permanently caucus with their chosen parties.

4. *The possibility and necessity of cooperation* — As part of the structures of the Progressive Congress, a Joint Policy Commission is formed. The chairpersons of the Commission are elected by Congress delegates, and its membership is elected from among candidates who represent the policy research branches of participating organisations. These are distributed so as to ensure representation for left organisations from across all parts of society (i.e., parties, trade unions, thinktanks, faith and denominational groups, education associations, etc.). The

purpose of the Commission is to find and develop the principled frameworks and procedures for left cooperation across social divides. As with the Progressive Congress, participation in the Joint Policy Commissions is voluntary but strongly incentivised.

5. *Methods of cooperation* — Every left organisation amends its rulebook or constitution to start with an explicit statement of its principles. This should clarify how the organisation intends to address its social concerns, and how it understands and aims to realise its core values. The same documents should also enshrine its preferred partners for future cooperation, both within and beyond its particular domain of societal activity. This may also include a list, in general terms, of the kinds of cooperative projects the organisation would be willing to jointly pursue with each of these partners.

6. *Past and future* — Every left organisation introduces a permanent truth and reconciliation commission within its structures. Its purpose is to quickly and transparently arbitrate complaints and crises that arise within the organisation, and correspond with the equivalent commissions in other organisations in cases where complaints have arisen between the organisations. To support stronger internal investigative and arbitration processes alongside more effective disciplinary mechanisms, the truth and reconciliation commission appoints a body of provosts for each organisation. The purpose of these provosts is to oversee and enforce the commission's decisions. The commissions are matched by an equivalent Truth and Reconciliation Forum hosted by the Progressive Congress.

7. *Personality and policy* — Every left organisation introduces mandatory periodic renomination and reselection processes for all elected organisational positions (e.g., parliamentary candidates, leadership, upper echelons). Nominations and selections are held on a 'faction list' system, so that candidates for each

position are designated as *Spitzenkandidaten* ('lead candidates') for a particular ideological grouping within the organisation. Each grouping determines its own list of 'substitute' candidates, who are 'bumped up' into the positions it wins as a faction if its *Spitzenkandidaten* are recalled for any reason (i.e., avoiding byelections for these positions). At the same time, organisations relax the requirements and lower the thresholds for votes of confidence and recall procedures to be launched against members in elected positions. This allows individuals to be removed without costing their ideological groupings the positions they have won.

8. *Protest and construction* — Every left organisation introduces a permanent audit and scrutiny commission within its structures. Its purpose is to monitor the activities of the agents who hold positions above a certain predefined level of seniority, for which the commission appoints a body of commissary scrutineers. The aim of this monitoring is to confirm whether senior organisational figures are using their roles to both pursue and prefigure projects of diagnosis, critique, and positive construction. These commissions are matched by an equivalent grassroots Audit and Scrutiny Forum at the level of the Progressive Congress, which is designed to allow for cross-ideological feedback and exchange to crowdsource 'best practice' between different left organisations' internal commissions and scrutineers.

9. *Discussion and decision* — With the support and facilitation of the Progressive Congress, left organisations simplify the formal appeal mechanisms and lower the threshold requirements for their ordinary members to call special, extraordinary, or emergency conferences. These can be conferences of the organisation's members, or *ad hoc* congresses of two or more left organisations. They can also be given several levels of gradation: not all conferences have to involve the entire organisation, but they can also lead to summoning its relevant bodies (e.g., executive committee, policy committee, etc.) for consultation and policy change.

10. *Unity in different forms* — Every left organisation formulates and internally settles a system of pre-agreements or preliminary expressions of intent to cooperate with specific other left organisations. The negotiations and discussions for these are conducted alongside the everyday other business of the organisation, both unofficially by ordinary members and officially by a body of appointed negotiators. The aim of this is to pre-empt moments where cooperation becomes urgent, and smooth the process of formalising the details of collaboration. In other words, left organisations transparently embrace what is known to happen already anyway at an informal and clandestine level, both between organisational leaderships and among their activists.

# FURTHER READING

It is extremely challenging to create even a moderately parsimonious definitive castlist of 'key thinkers' or 'key works' for the left. Many radicals of many ideological persuasions have made their contributions over the centuries to the inchwise onward march of progress. But perhaps a promising place to start is the selection of figures I named at the start of chapter 10 as having summed up most effectively some aspect of the thinking and experience of 'those without'.

Karl Marx (1818-1883) and his lifelong collaborator Friedrich Engels (1820-1895) are arguably the thinkers who have made the single greatest contribution to left ideology. Their manifold writings and correspondence can be found in the 50 volumes of *Collected Works* (London: Lawrence and Wishart, 1975-2004), of which perhaps the most important are *The Communist Manifesto* (1848), *Capital* (3 vols., 1867-94), *The Eighteenth Brumaire of Louis Napoleon* (1852), and *Critique of the Gotha Programme* (1875).

Of their many intellectual successors, two who left an especially lasting legacy on the dividing lines within the left are Eduard Bernstein (1850-1932) and Rosa Luxemburg (1871-1919). They were the main spokespeople for 'reformist' and 'revolutionary' tendencies in socialist thought, which ultimately laid the foundations for the split between social democracy and communism. For Bernstein, the key text is *Preconditions of Socialism* (Cambridge: Cambridge University Press, 1993 [1899]), as well as three volumes of later texts: Marius S. Ostrowski (ed.), *Eduard Bernstein on Social Democracy and International Politics: Essays and Other Writings* (Basingstoke: Palgrave Macmillan, 2018), *Eduard Bernstein on the German Revolution: Selected Historical Writings* (Basingstoke: Palgrave Macmillan, 2019), and *Eduard Bernstein on Socialism Past and Present: Essays and Lectures* (Basingstoke: Palgrave Macmillan, 2020). For Luxemburg, there is an ongoing project to publish her *Complete Works* (London: Verso, 2014-) in 14 volumes, of which the key texts are *Social Reform or Revolution?* (1900), *The Mass Strike, the Political Party and the Trade Unions* (1906), *The Accumulation of Capital* (1913), and *The Junius Pamphlet* (1915).

In the liberal corner, one of the greatest contributions comes from the debate between John Dewey (1859-1952) and Walter Lippmann (1889-1974) on the relationship between the elite and the mass in contemporary democracies. Both were highly prolific, publishing books at a prodigious rate throughout the 1910s to the 1950s, which helped frame a distinctive new strand of American progressive liberalism. There is a 38-volume series available of Dewey's *Collected Works* (Carbondale, IL: Southern Illinois University Press, 2008), of which the key texts are *The Public and its Problems* (1927), *Individualism Old and New* (1930), *Liberalism and Social Action* (1935), and *Freedom and Culture* (1939). For Lippmann, the central texts are *Public Opinion* (New York, NY: Harcourt, Brace & Co., 1922), *The Phantom Public* (Piscataway, NJ: Transaction Publishers, 1925), *The Good Society* (New York, NY: Atlantic Monthly Press, 1937), and *The Public Philosophy* (New York, NY: New American Library, 1955).

The Pankhursts were a family intimately associated with the different ideological strands of the suffrage movement in the UK, comprising the socialist (later conservative) Emmeline (1858-1928), the conservative-liberal Christabel (1880-1958), and the communist Sylvia (1882-1960). For some of their key texts, see Emmeline

Pankhurst, *My Own Story* (London: Virago Ltd., 1979 [1914]); Christabel Pankhurst, *Pressing Problems of the Closing Age* (London: Morgan & Scott Ltd., 1924), *The World's Unrest: Visions of the Dawn* (London: Morgan & Scott Ltd., 1926), and *Unshackled: The Story of How We Won the Vote* (London: Hutchinson & Co., 1959); and Kathryn Dodd (ed.), *A Sylvia Pankhurst Reader* (Manchester: Manchester University Press, 1993), especially the selections from *The Suffragette: The History of the Women's Militant Suffrage Movement* (London: Gay & Hancock, 1911), *The Suffragette Movement: An Intimate Account of Persons and Ideals* (London: Chatto & Windus, 1984 [1931]), and *Non-Leninist Marxism: Writings on the Workers Councils* (St Petersburg, FL: Red and Black Publishers, 2007).

Betty Friedan (1921-2006) and Judith Butler (1956-) are in many respects among the Pankhursts' most influential successors in subsequent waves of feminist thought. Friedan's seminal text is *The Feminine Mystique* (New York, NY: W.W. Norton & Co., 1963), which is often held up as one of the key catalysts for 'second wave' feminism, and which she later followed with books including *The Second Stage* (New York, NY: Abacus, 1981) and *Beyond Gender* (Princeton, NJ: Woodrow Wilson Center Press, 1997). For Butler, the major text is *Gender Trouble: Feminism and the Subversion of Identity* (New York, NY: Routledge, 1990), with other significant contributions in such works as *Bodies that Matter: On the discursive limits of 'sex'* (New York, NY: Routledge, 1993), *Excitable Speech: A Politics of the Performative* (New York, NY: Routledge, 1997), and *Undoing Gender* (New York, NY: Routledge, 2004).

Frantz Fanon (1925-1961) and Mahatma Gandhi (1869-1948) are two of the most influential figures in anti-colonial thought, whose legacy has inspired and informed opponents of white supremacism and European global domination in many regions of the world. Fanon's two key texts are *Black Skin, White Masks* (New York, NY: Grove Press, 1967 [1952]) and *The Wretched of the Earth* (New York, NY: Grove Weidenfeld, 1963 [1961]), with some further significant contributions in *A Dying Colonialism* (New York,

NY: Grove Press, 1965 [1959]) and *Toward the African Revolution* (New York, Grove Press, 1969 [1964]). There is a 100-volume set of Gandhi's *Collected Works* (New Delhi: Publications Division, Ministry of Information and Broadcasting, Govt. of India, 1994), of which the most important texts are *Hind Swaraj* (1909) and *Satyagraha in South Africa* (1928).

Lastly, Kimberlé Crenshaw (1959-) is one of the leading modern exponents of critical race theory, and the originator of the concept of 'intersectionality', whose key texts can be found in *On Intersectionality: Essential Writings* (New York, NY: New Press, 2017).

More generally, the nature of the left and its history have been retrodden many times and in many different shades. Among the best overviews are Sheri Berman, *The Primacy of Politics: Social Democracy and the Making of Europe's Twentieth Century* (Cambridge: Cambridge University Press, 2006); Donald Sassoon, *One Hundred Years of Socialism: The West European Left in the Twentieth Century* (London: I.B. Tauris, 2013); and Darrow Schecter, *The History of the Left from Marx to the Present: Theoretical Perspectives* (London: Bloomsbury, 2007).

For overviews of the theory and history of the ideologies typically associated with the left, see John Barry, *Rethinking Green Politics: Nature, Virtue, and Progress* (London: SAGE, 1998); Edmund Fawcett, *Liberalism: The Life of an Idea* (Princeton, NJ: Princeton University Press, 2014); Michael Freeden, Lyman Tower Sargent, and Marc Stears (eds.), *The Oxford Handbook of Political Ideologies* (Oxford: Oxford University Press, 2015); Vincent Geoghegan (ed.), *Political Ideologies* (Abingdon: Routledge, 2014); Axel Honneth, *The Idea of Socialism: Towards a Renewal* (Cambridge: Polity, 2017); Peter Marshall, *Demanding the Impossible: A History of Anarchism* (London: HarperCollins, 1992); and Thomas Meyer, *The Theory of Social Democracy* (Cambridge: Polity, 2007).

Left approaches to history and historiography typically centre the role of the downtrodden and dispossessed within narratives often dominated by conquerors and other elites. Some centre the role of the working class in world history, such as Geoff Eley and Keith H. Nield, *The Future of Class in History: What's Left of the Social?* (Ann Arbor, MI: University of Michigan Press, 2007); Neil Faulkner, *A Marxist History of the World: From Neanderthals to Neoliberals* (London: Pluto Press, 2013); or Karl Heinz Roth (ed.), *On the Road to Global Labour History* (Chicago, IL: Haymarket Books, 2018).

Gender historians, postcolonial historians, and queer historians respectively address the major events and protagonists of global history through alternative dimensions of struggle and disadvantage. For gender history, some excellent examples are Laura Lee Downs, *Writing Gender History* (London: Bloomsbury, 2010); Susan Kingsley Kent, *Gender and History* (Basingstoke: Palgrave, 2011); Sonya O. Rose, *What is Gender History?* (Cambridge: Polity, 2010); and Joan Wallach Scott (ed.), *Gender and the Politics of History* (New York, NY: Columbia University Press, 1999).

For postcolonial history see, for instance, Samir Amin, *Global History: A View from the South* (Cape Town: Pambazuka Press, 2011); Dipesh Chakrabarty, *Provincializing Europe: Postcolonial Thought and Historical Difference* (Princeton, NJ: Princeton University Press, 2007); Partha Chatterjee, *The Nation and its Fragments: Colonial and Postcolonial Histories* (Princeton, NJ: Princeton University Press, 1993); Rosalind Morris (ed.), *Can the Subaltern Speak?: Reflections on the History of an Idea* (New York, NY: Columbia University Press, 2010); and Edward Saïd, *Orientalism* (London: Routledge & Kegan Paul, 1978).

For some leading examples of the still-nascent field of queer history, see Michael Bronski, *A Queer History of the United States* (Boston, MA: Beacon Press, 2011); Brian Lewis (ed.), *British Queer History: New Approaches and Perspectives* (Manchester: Manchester University Press, 2013); and Susan Stryker, *Transgender History: The Roots of Today's Revolution* (New York, NY: Seal Press, 2017).

There has been much philosophical engagement with the left's core concepts from a variety of traditions, with perhaps the best formal overview being Jonathan Wolff and Avner de-Shalit,

*Disadvantage* (Oxford: Oxford University Press, 2007). By way of an introduction to the myriad different understandings of power, see Mark Haugaard (ed.), *Power: A Reader* (Manchester: Manchester University Press, 2002); Clarissa Rile Hayward, *De-facing Power* (Cambridge: Cambridge University Press, 2000); Steven Lukes (ed.), *Power* (New York, NY: New York University Press, 1986; and Thomas Wartenberg (ed.), *Rethinking Power* (Albany, NY: State University of New York Press, 1992).

On the place of structures in society, see Pierre Bourdieu, *Outline of a Theory of Practice* (Cambridge: Cambridge University Press, 1977); Michel Foucault, *Discipline and Punish: The Birth of the Prison* (New York, NY: Pantheon Books, 1977 [1975]); Anthony Giddens, *The Constitution of Society: Outline of the Theory of Structuration* (Cambridge: Polity, 1984); Richard Merton, *Social Theory and Social Structure* (New York, NY: Free Press, 1957); and Talcott Parsons, *The Structure of Social Action* (New York, NY: McGraw-Hill, 1937).

For a range of key texts on recognition and anti-discrimination, see Wendy Brown, *States of Injury* (Princeton, NJ: Princeton University Press, 1995); Judith Butler and Gayatri Chakravorty Spivak, *Who Sings the Nation-State?* (New York, NY: Seagull Books, 2007); Axel Honneth and Nancy Fraser (eds.), *Redistribution or Recognition? A political-philosophical exchange* (London: Verso, 2003); Lois McNay, *Against Recognition* (Cambridge: Polity, 2008); and Charles Taylor, *Multiculturalism and the Politics of Recognition* (Princeton, NJ: Princeton University Press, 1994).

On cooperation, see Garrett Cullity, *Concern, Respect, and Cooperation* (Oxford: Oxford University Press, 2018); Michael Tomasello, *Why We Cooperate* (Cambridge, MA: MIT Press, 2009); and Tom R. Tyler, *Why People Cooperate: The Role of Social Motivations* (Princeton, NJ: Princeton University Press, 2011).

Similarly, the left's values have come under intense scrutiny in academic thought, especially within the sub-disciplines of social and political theory. On equality, see John Baker *et al.*, *Equality: From Theory to Action* (Basingstoke: Palgrave Macmillan, 2004); Andrew

Mason (ed.), *Ideals of Equality* (Oxford: Blackwell, 1998); Louis P. Pojman and Robert Westmoreland, *Equality: Selected Readings* (Oxford: Oxford University Press, 1997); and Stuart White, *Equality* (Cambridge: Polity, 2006).

For justice, see Brian Barry, *Why Social Justice Matters* (Cambridge: Polity, 2005); Amartya Sen, *The Idea of Justice* (London: Penguin, 2009); Michael Walzer, *Spheres of Justice* (New York, NY: Basic Books, 1983); and Iris Marion Young, *Justice and the Politics of Difference* (Princeton, NJ: Princeton University Press, 1990).

On solidarity, see Keith Banting and Will Kymlicka (eds.), *The Strains of Commitment: The Political Sources of Solidarity in Diverse Societies* (Oxford: Oxford University Press, 2017); Lilie Chouliaraki, *The Ironic Spectator: Solidarity in the Age of Post-Humanitarianism* (Cambridge: Polity, 2012); Sally J. Scholz, *Political Solidarity* (University Park, PA: Penn State University Press, 2008); and Tommie Shelby, *We Who Are Dark: The Philosophical Foundations of Black Solidarity* (Cambridge, MA: Harvard University Press, 2007).

For freedom, see Ian Carter, Matthew Kramer, & Hillel Steiner (eds.), *Freedom: A Philosophical Anthology* (Oxford: Blackwell, 2006); John Gray & Zbigniew Pełczy ski, *Conceptions of liberty in political philosophy* (New York, NY: St. Martin's Press, 1984); Quentin Skinner, *Liberty before Liberalism* (Cambridge: Cambridge University Press, 1998); and Radoslav Selucký, *Marxism, socialism, freedom* (London: Macmillan, 1979).

On pluralism, see William E. Connolly, *Pluralism* (Durham, NC: Duke University Press, 2005); Peter Lassman, *Pluralism* (Cambridge: Polity, 2011); Jacob T. Levy, *Rationalism, Pluralism, and Freedom* (Oxford: Oxford University Press, 2017); and Chantal Mouffe (ed.), *Dimensions of Radical Democracy: Pluralism, Citizenship, Community* (London: Verso, 1992).

And for progress, see Jeffrey C. Alexander and Piotr Sztompka, *Rethinking Progress: Movements, Forces, and Ideas at the End of the 20$^{th}$ Century* (Boston, MA: Unwin Hyman, 1990); Carlo

Bordoni, *Hubris and Progress* (Abingdon: Routledge, 2019); Marc Fleurbaey *et al.*, *A Manifesto for Social Progress* (Cambridge: Cambridge University Press, 2018); and Arthur M. Melzer, Jerry Weinberger, and M. Richard Zinman (eds.), *History and the Idea of Progress* (Ithaca, NY: Cornell University Press, 1995).

Finally, there have been a host of brilliant contributions from various strands of social theory to considering questions of personal identity and the domains of societal activity. On what is too often loosely termed 'identity politics', perhaps the most wide-ranging and insightful sources are Lisa Heldke and Peg O'Connor (eds.), *Oppression, Privilege and Resistance: Theoretical Perspectives on Racism, Sexism, and Heterosexism* (Boston, MA: McGraw-Hill, 2004); Margaret Kohn and Keally McBride, *Political Theories of Decolonization: Postcolonialism and the Problem of Foundations* (Oxford: Oxford University Press, 2011); Chandra Talpade Mohanty, *Feminism Without Borders: Decolonizing Theory, Practicing Solidarity* (Durham, NC: Duke University Press, 2003); Uma Narayan and Sandra Harding (eds.), *Decentering the Center: Philosophy for a Multicultural, Postcolonial, and Feminist World* (Bloomington, IN: Indiana University Press, 2000); and George Yancy (ed.), *Reframing the Practice of Philosophy: Bodies of Color, Bodies of Knowledge* (Albany, NY: State University of New York Press, 2012).

On the nature and interrelationship of societal domains, see Louis Althusser, *On the Reproduction of Capitalism: Ideology and Ideological State Apparatuses* (London: Verso, 2014 [1971]); Ernest Gellner, *Plough, Sword and Book: The Structure of Human History* (London: Collins Harvill, 1988); Michael Mann, *The Sources of Social Power, vol.1: A History of Power from the Beginning to AD1760* (Cambridge: Cambridge University Press, 1986); Göran Therborn, *The Ideology of Power and the Power of Ideology* (London: Verso, 1980); and John B. Thompson, *The Media and Modernity: A Social Theory of the Media* (Cambridge: Polity, 1995).